Presented To:

_____

From:

_____

Date:

_____

The Eye of a Needle

When Life Looks Impossible

Jeff Scurlock

Destiny Vine Books

All rights reserved.
First Edition Copyright © 2012 Jeff Scurlock

ISBN – 13:978-0615608167
ISBN-10:0615608167

Destiny Vine Books

All scripture quotations, unless otherwise indicated, are taken from the Holy Bible, New International Version, NIV. Copyrith 1973, 1978,1984, 2011 by BBiblica, Inc. Used by permission of Zondervan. All rights reserved worldwide. www.zondervan.com

Scripture taken from the Holy Bible, New King James Version, Copyright 1982 by Thomas Nelson, INC. Used by permission. All Rights Reserved.

Scripture quotations from THE MESSAGE. Copyright, by Eugene H. Peterson 1993, 1994, 1995, 1996, 2000, 2001, 2002. Used by permission of NavPress Publishing Group.

Destiny Vine Books is the publishing arm of Jeff Scurlock ministries.

All rights reserved. No part of this book may be reproduced or transmitted in any form or by any means, electronic or mechanical, including photocopying and recording, or by any information storage and retrieval system, without permission in writing from the author.

Editor: Renee Shipp
Author Photo: Becky Dykes

THANK YOU

To Felicia: Thank you for the push you gave me, for encouragement and for being patient through this process.

To Renee Shipp who did my editing: there are not enough words to express how grateful I am to you. Your hard work and continual words of encouragement have been a tremendous blessing to me.

To my church family who encouraged me: I would list names but most assuredly I would leave someone out. You know who you are.

DEDICATION

This book is dedicated first of all to God. Without Him I can do nothing. Any glory from my writing belongs to Him.

To my beautiful wife Felicia, who is my best friend, the mother of our three beautiful children, and my ministry and life partner.

To my awesome kids who are all grown up now: Adam, Kara and Lauren. You bring joy into my life.

To my parents, Charles and Naomi Scurlock

To Felicia's Parents, Sam and Doris Wright

To my grandchildren who are yet to be born (first one is on the way). This book is part of my legacy to you. Always believe God for big things. He won't let you down.

Table of Contents

    Preface

    Introduction

1	Nothing Is Impossible	17
2	Determination	29
3	Noah	39
4	David Ring	47
5	Sarah	55
6	Dave Roever	65
7	Abraham	71
8	Bill McDonald	77
9	Abraham, Part II	85
10	Joseph	99
11	Deborah Ford	111
12	Paul and Silas	123
13	Shadrach, Meshach and Abednego	133
14	Failure	145
15	Faith	155
16	Challenges	163
17	Help is on the way.	171
18	How?	177

    Conclusion

Preface

Since I was in Junior High School I've wanted to write. It began when I read my first book cover to cover. It was a novel on a junior high level called *Pilot Jack Knight*. Reading that book caused me to fall in love with reading and being creative with words.

For whatever reason other than blogging, I've not fulfilled that dream until now.

Over lunch one day I mentioned to Felicia (my wife), that I wanted to write a book. As I said it, I broke into unexpected tears. I attempted to hide my face from others in the restaurant. Felicia said, "Well, honey, do it." It was the push I needed. Felicia has always been supportive of my dreams. I love her for many reasons. One is that she encourages me.

That day, after lunch, I immediately sat down at my computer and began the manuscript to the book that you are holding in your hand.

The words came easily. It was like God took control of my hands. I don't give Him credit for the spelling errors and typos, but I do give Him the credit for the message. If there is any praise to come out of this book, it belongs to Him.

My prayer is that as you read this book, your faith will be aroused, that you will find a determination in your life that you may have lost or possibly never had.

I want you to have big faith; to face challenges, obstacles and the call of God with confidence, knowing that with God, all things are possible.

Introduction

How many times in your life have you used the word *impossible*? How many times have you thrown it out carelessly in a conversation as a way of avoiding even the slightest challenge? Do we really stop and consider the power of our words when we throw them about like a plaything? The truth is that words hold power.

"Death and life are in the power of the tongue, and those who love it will eat its fruit.[1]

Have you considered that when you tell your children "it can't be done; it's impossible," that your words may be killing a dream? Proverbs says that "those who love it will eat its fruit." Love what? Life or Death! Maybe we should really reconsider how we use the word "impossible" and,

---

[1] Proverbs 18:21

when we do use it, to make sure we disclaim *that* statement with the following statement: "but with God all things are possible."

Don't tell your children that it's impossible for them to make the team. Don't speak negative about others' dreams and aspirations. Don't make it a habit of tearing down dreams with your words. Be a builder. Tell those around you that you believe in them and that you know that with their determination and God's help that anything is possible. If your initial response tends to be negative, hold your peace, think about what you are about to say and then speak faith. If someone is believing for something big, your encouragement may be invaluable to them.

If you're the one with the dream, stay away from dream killers. Don't listen to those who are negative or don't believe in you. When they do get a negative word in, replace it with faith.

Impossible is defined by dictionary.com as "not possible; unable to be, exist, happen, etc. Unable to be done, performed, effected, etc., not to be done, endured, etc., with any degree of reason or propriety: an impossible situation. Utterly impracticable:[2] In this book

I'm going to use scripture and life stories that will rekindle the flames of your faith and remind you that nothing is impossible. Nothing is impossible when determination is coupled together with faith. Nothing is impossible when you say what you believe and believe what you say. When you live what you believe and put action behind your words, nothing is impossible.

We should all be challenged. I am challenged as I write this book to believe more, to accomplish more.

I'm going to use words like "dream", "big" and "possible" to describe that thing God is calling you to do or that thing you've always

---

[2] Dictionary.com

wanted to accomplish. It might not be literally impossible but it might be so BIG that it looks impossible. My point is this: Whether I use "possible," dream or big, the outcome of your situation all depends on your determination, your faith and your confidence in God and the promises of his Word.

When someone tells you that it can't happen, that you shouldn't try with any reasonable expectation of success, or that it's utterly impracticable, you tell them that in the Kingdom of God, *nothing is impossible*. Those who say it's impossible should get out of the way of those who are doing.

Chapter One
Nothing Is Impossible

And when they had come to the multitude, a man came to Him, kneeling down to Him and saying,

"Lord, have mercy on my son, for he is an epileptic and suffers severely; for he often falls into the fire and often into the water. So I brought him to Your disciples, but they could not cure him."[3]

"They could not cure him." That's not such a horrible thing. After all this boy has epilepsy and epilepsy was an incurable disease. Over two thousand years later, epilepsy is treatable but still no cure.

---

[3] Matthew 17:14-16

In other words, if the man in the story took his son to a physician of his day or a physician of the twenty-first century and asked that physician to cure his son, the physician would have said "It's IMPOSSIBLE." If it's impossible for the medical world, what are a few fishermen turned followers of Jesus supposed to do?

At this point you would expect that Jesus would give his disciples a pat on the back and words of encouragement. You would expect that He would say something like "that's ok boys; after all it is epilepsy! Hang in there boys. Sooner or later someone will come with a request that is reasonable!" Jesus' response was quite different than what human reason would expect. He actually came down hard on the guys. My daughters would say that He "snapped on the disciples." Jesus responded to the man's words with strong words for His disciples.

"O faithless and perverse generation"[4]

"WHAT? Did He say what I think He said? Did He just say we are a faithless and perverse generation? Does He realize that this boy has epilepsy? Does He know that we tried, and still He calls us faithless and perverse? That's a little harsh. We're His disciples. We've heard every sermon, we've seen every miracle. We are charter members of his church and we are a faithless and perverse generation?"

What would Jesus say to the church of the twenty first century? Would He call us faithless and perverse? When is the last time you cured (by faith) someone with a disease? I'm just asking. This paragraph is not intended to be judgmental in any way. I'm just pointing out the fact that Jesus came down hard on His disciples because of the lack of faith they were demonstrating. Maybe we should take a hard look at our faith. We should work at not only saying we have faith, but in demonstrating faith.

---

[4] Matthew 17:16

Have you considered the fact that God might want to do something really big through your life? In considering it, have you considered that in order for something big to happen, you might just need to demonstrate a little bit of faith?

It seems to me that the church in the United States has decided to go the easy route. It's easier to make excuses. I've heard some say that Jesus never intended for us to cure the sick like the disciples were supposed to do. Really? Can you back that up with the Word? Others say that miracles died out with the original apostles. It's nothing but excuses. Reading the story of the paralytic, I'm stirred by the fact that Jesus expects His people to operate beyond what is considered possible; to reach for things that "normal" people say are impossible.

The church in the United States is coasting on easy street. Disciples show up for one, maybe two service a week at their church. They sit on padded seats in air-conditioned buildings happy to get out in time to beat the crowd to the local restaurant and frustrated if the service goes a few minutes too long. For the most part, we don't want to be bothered by fasting, prayer meetings and faith to move mountains. And we certainly don't want to be bothered by ANYTHING that takes us out of our comfort zones. That's right, comfort zones: the safe place where some insist on living their lives.

It's easy to coast through life and do the easy thing. That's not what God has called us to do. God has called us to believe Him for the hard thing, the seemingly impossible thing and for the absolutely impossible thing.

The story goes on. Later, in private, the disciples asked Jesus why they couldn't cure the boy. Let's pick it back up:

Then the disciples came to Jesus privately and said, "Why could we not cast it out?" So Jesus said to them, "Because of your unbelief; [5]

---

[5] Matthew 17:19-20

Unbelief stops everything. It's like the parking brake on a car. The engine is running and the transmission is in gear. The accelerator is pressed but this car is going nowhere with the brake on. Unbelief stops even natural endeavors.

As a young boy and teenager, I was very involved in athletics. I started playing football in the second grade and played all the way through high school graduation. I was part of the track and field team as well as the weight-lifting team. I did go out for basketball one time, but since this book is not intended to be comic relief, we won't go there.

There are many important aspects to playing the game of football: Strength, speed, agility and technique, to name a few. After spending years playing football and many more years watching the game, I believe the most important aspect of successful football is believing. A football coach not only has to work his players hard in order for them to get stronger, faster and know their technique, he also has to make believers out of them. That's why most coaches give a motivational speech just before the team takes the field. They do it to make sure they still believe. Many college and professional sports teams employ the services of a sports psychologist. The purpose is to help their players to be believers. It's just that important. They have to believe.

When my son, Adam, was in High School, he attended a small school in Florida. This school had one of the most successful football teams I have ever followed. Here's the kicker: the team was always small; by small I mean physically and numerically. Rarely were there any boys on the team that possessed great physical stature. This team rarely had more than twenty to twenty-five players dressed out for the game. Since it was a small school, the team did play teams from other small schools. Those teams didn't stand a chance. Games would get ugly and lopsided. This small school football team also played teams from big schools. It wasn't unusual for this coach to schedule games with teams from much bigger schools. Those teams would strut onto the field with their huge players and large numbers of boys thinking that this little team would be easy taking. That wasn't the case. Most of the time, that little team would take teams with fifty or even seventy players to the woodshed. The same players from those teams who strutted onto the field looking confident would leave with heads down in disbelief.

What was so unique about this small team from a small school that made them so successful? They believed. It had to be that. I looked at and considered every possibility for the success of that team. There was no other logical explanation. That coach had a unique ability of convincing his little team that they could beat anyone and most of the time, they did.

Many people rarely experience real victory in their lives. They look at the large obstacles that strut onto the field of life and they cower in fear. They have never been told they could overcome obstacles in their lives. As a matter of fact, many grew up in homes with parents that never attempted anything past the mundane rituals of life and were told by those same parents how stupid they were. The truth is that there are many people who have made Jesus the Lord of their lives who have never believed God for something beyond their previous experiences, family traditions or curses.

Through the years, I've watched believers cower from any challenge in life because of fear, intimidation and the absolute lack of faith that something big or even impossible could happen in their lives. It's just easier to not believe. It's easier to make excuses. It's easier to be lazy.

Jesus didn't say you had to have huge faith! He said just have a little faith and "nothing will be impossible to you."

Why am I mingling theology with stories of natural ability and accomplishment? Because I'm convinced that believing in yourself as a child of God and the abilities that He has give you and believing that God can use your abilities are a recipe for big things in your life. I also want you to know that if you lack ability, that God will honor your faith. Big things will happen.

I should also point out that in the story; Jesus never said that you must have faith and ability. He said you need faith.

Now faith is the substance of things hoped for, the evidence of things not seen.[6]

- Faith believes for something you can't see, touch, feel or taste with the natural senses.
- Faith is the willingness to look foolish to others.
- **Faith is jumping off a cliff thousands of feet from the bottom of a canyon and trusting that a piece of material is going to pop out when you pull the string, slow down your descent and land you safely on the ground.**
- Faith is doing something that seems unreasonable with the assurance that God has spoken to you.
- Faith is demonstrating complete confidence in the Word of God.
- Faith is Hope!

I heard a humorous story of some nuns who years ago ran out of gas traveling to a nursing home with some supplies. Because there was a gas station within sight, they began rummaging through the car for something to put gas into. The only thing they found was a bed pan. Knowing that they only needed to start the car and drive a short distance to the station, they decided that the bed pan would do just fine. They walked to the station and

---

[6] Hebrews 11:1 NKJV

purchased as much gas as that bed pan would hold. When they arrived back at the car, using a funnel the gas station attendant loaned them, they began pouring the gas from the bed pan into the car. While they were doing this, a "faith preacher" drove by. Seeing the nuns pouring the contents of the bed pan into the car the preacher said, "NOW THAT'S FAITH!"

Faith is putting your trust in God for everything from healing the sick to helping you with your goals in life. The key is believing.

As a high school-power lifter, I had to be strong and I had to believe. To lift huge amounts of weight you not only have to train, you have to be able to convince yourself that it could be done.

I knew what it meant to believe. As a teenager my pastor was not only a great preacher, he was an excellent motivational speaker to athletes. He served as the chaplain of our football team and I heard him preach the stories of the Bible to athletes. He convinced us that anything was possible, if we would only believe.

In 1977, there were no high school athletes in my county that could bench press 300 pounds. Today, it's common, but in the seventies it was almost unheard of in our part of the country.

I'll never forget a certain weight-lifting meet. I told those who prepared the weights for the attempt that my attempt would be 300 pounds. To that point, I had never lifted 300 pounds; not even in training. I heard a few gasps and the rumble of conversation from the spectators about my upcoming attempt. I'm not telling you that for me to bench 300 pounds was an impossible feat. I was strong and I had worked hard. This attempt was the result of hours and hours of weight-training. It was, however, a threshold that I had never attempted to break before and a threshold that none of the other young men were even close to breaking. I believed I could do it. I'd been working hard. If I had not believed, I'm sure I wouldn't have tried.

Had I tried without confidence, I'm sure I would have failed. I was successful in my attempt. I was thronged by my teammates. My dad sat in the bleachers with a proud look. It was a great night for me. *It was great* because I reaped the benefits of hard work and I believed.

What in the world does that story have to do with this book? The memory of that weight-lifting meet encourages me to believe for other things, even thirty-five years later.

Unbelief hinders everything when it comes to a relationship with God. **Belief** or **Faith** is the very foundation of how we know God.

That if you confess with your mouth, "Jesus is Lord," and believe in your heart that God raised him from the dead, you will be saved. For it is with your heart that you believe and are justified..,[7]

We can't even start a relationship with God without believing and we are certainly not going to accomplish feats for the Kingdom of God that are thought to be impossible without believing.

After rebuking his disciples for their lack of faith and for their inability to heal the epileptic boy, Jesus continued with some good news.

"For assuredly, I say to you, if you have faith as a mustard seed, you will say to this mountain, 'Move from here to there,' and it will move; and nothing will be impossible for you." [8]

The mustard seed is not to be confused with the mustard greens that we grow and eat in the southern United States and other places. That mustard of my experience is a green leafy plant that grows for a short time. The leaves are harvested, cleaned and cooked with lots of bacon grease. My grandparents and parents taught me to love mustard greens and as I sit here writing I'm getting really hungry.......

---

[7] Matthew 17:20-21
[8] Matthew 21:21

The plant referred to here is generally considered to be black mustard, a large annual plant up to 9 feet tall, but growing from a proverbially small seed.[9]

The point is, Jesus said that if you have just a little bit of faith, even if it's just the size of a mustard seed, that you could move mountains and that nothing will be impossible for you. Did you get it? *Nothing* will be impossible for you! I want you to be challenged and encouraged. Chances are, you're facing a dilemma or multiple dilemmas.

Whatever you do, please don't stop reading this book. Stay with it all the way through. I believe you will be encouraged. You will be encouraged to believe.

In the last few years, our economy has been poor; and that's putting it lightly. Many have lost jobs or been forced to take pay cuts. The housing market has crashed because folks can't pay the mortgage and the market has become saturated with empty houses for sale. Because there are so many of these empty houses with "for sale" signs in front of them, these houses have lost large parts of their previous value. Because of this crash in the real estate market, those who need to sell their homes due to a cut in pay or the loss of a job can't do so. Thus, another family forfeits on a mortgage and it goes on and on.

Confidence in the economy is low. Those who have money are reluctant to spend it and everything suffers. Money is the life-blood of an economy, and if that blood isn't flowing, the result is not good. Can you believe God for a financial miracle even in the middle of a recession?

God is not subject to man's economy. Jesus said that all you need is a little faith. Yes, I do understand that scripture teaches us to put work with our faith. I'm not advocating a hyper-spiritual conduct that causes someone

---

[9] http://www.enwikipedia.org/wiki/parableofthemustardseed

to stay home when they could be working. What I am telling you is that God will honor your effort, but you need to mix faith with your effort.

In the discussion of the impossible, I must include the following story. It's so important to the theme of this book that my title came from it. It's not really necessary that I include the whole story, but I will, just to make sure that you don't doubt my conclusion by thinking that I have not been true to the context of the scripture.

Now a man came up to Jesus and asked,

"Teacher, what good thing must I do to get eternal life?"

"Why do you ask me about what is good?" Jesus replied. "There is only One who is good. If you want to enter life, obey the commandments.

"Which ones?" the man inquired. Jesus replied,

"'Do not murder, do not commit adultery, do not steal, do not give false testimony, honor your father and mother,' and 'love your neighbor as yourself." All these I have kept," the young man said. "What do I still lack?" Jesus answered, "If you want to be perfect, go, sell your possessions and give to the poor, and you will have treasure in heaven. Then come, follow me." When the young man heard this he went away sad, because he had great wealth. Then Jesus said to his disciples, "I tell you the truth, it is hard for a rich man to enter the kingdom of heaven.

Again I tell you, it is easier for a camel to go through the eye of a needle than for a rich man to enter the kingdom of God."

When the disciples heard this, they were greatly astonished and asked,

"Who then can be saved?"

Jesus looked at them and said, "With man this is impossible, *but with God all things are possible.*"[10]

---

[10] Matthew 19:16-26

Matthew, Mark and Luke each give their account of this conversation between this apparently rich man and Jesus. It's not my intention to break down the whole text and discuss the issue of rich men and heaven. Nor do I intend to discuss or debate whether or not there was a gate called the eye of the needle. What I want to point out is Jesus' declaration: "with man this is impossible, but not with God; ALL THINGS ARE POSSIBLE WITH GOD."

Back to the economy, I recently had a contractor say something really interesting to me. He said, "Jeff, if it wasn't for churches, my business would be bankrupt." What a testimony to God's economy. In a time when very few houses, stores or factories are being built, the churches who believe that anything is possible with God are going forward, expanding facilities and acting like the economy is great. It's because they understand God's economy. God's economy is great. *In God's economy, all things are possible.*

Quit looking at your natural circumstances. Look to the words of Jesus. Get the Word of God in your life and believe what it says. Yes, you can do what others think is impossible. You can believe God for the "Big Things" and see them come to pass. Yes, a camel can go through the eye of a needle when God is involved. Just believe.

Chapter Two
Determination

Determination is a powerful force in the life of someone who believes even in their own ability to achieve. History is replete with stories of individuals who overcame impossible situations to become successful far beyond what anyone thought was possible. They dream, they work hard, and they succeed.

Throughout this book, I will weave some awesome stories from scripture with modern-day stories of victory. We will talk about those who refused to let negative circumstances determine their future. You will read stories of a few modern-day men and women who achieved big, daunting tasks in the face of discouragement, apparent failure and grief over loss.

They are people who refused to quit, refused to turn back, and refused to accept defeat. There are people in history who have gotten the camel through the eye of a needle because they trusted God.

"I can do everything through him who gives me strength."[11]

Notice Paul's wording. I CAN DO. This is not a sit on your backside, doing-nothing-and-waiting-for-God-to-do-something mentality. This is having the determination to do, while relying on the strength of God to get it done. Determination defined: "the act of coming to a decision or of fixing or settling a purpose."[12]

What are the areas of your life in which determination just might come in handy? What are those seemingly impossible situations that you're facing that right now some good ole got-my-mind-made-up determination would benefit? Are you trying to quit smoking, lose some weight, start a business or even accomplish something really big in the Kingdom of God? This book is written with you in mind. Understand that just because something looks impossible on the surface doesn't necessarily mean that it is. Understand that even if it really is impossible, it's possible with God.

In the early days of the United States space program, scientists were just dreaming of men going into the earth's orbit and returning safely to the earth. Those dreams turned into pressure when the Russian space program put a man into a full orbit of the earth. The United States succeeded in putting a man in orbit, but the craft did not make a full orbit. The United States was embarrassed that they were behind in the space race to a country they believed was inferior.

The thought of going to the moon would have been laughable.

---

[11] Philippians 4:13
[12] Dictionary.com

It was in the context of this embarrassment that on May 25, 1961, President John F Kennedy boldly declared in a speech before a joint session of Congress that before the end of the decade, the United States would send men to the surface of the moon and then have them return safely home.[13]

July 20, 1969, less than six months before the end of the decade, Apollo 11 Commander Neil Armstrong and Edwin "Buzz" Aldrin, Jr. set their lunar module in the Sea of Tranquility on the surface of the moon. [14]

President Kennedy set the bar high and the men and women of the United States Space Agency went to work. They had a goal and a time frame. They were determined.

Has God placed a dream in your heart that you struggle with? Do you struggle with it because it looks so daunting? Do you measure the dream by what you think your natural abilities are? Does your dream look wonderful but impossible? Keep reading!

President Kennedy said in his speech that the "reason we are going to the moon is not because it's easy, but because it's hard."[15] Do you struggle with the fear that the dream might take too much effort and that you really don't think you have the ability to make it happen? Don't struggle with the dream. Put the dream in God's hands and then put steps behind your faith. God specializes in hard. *Fly to the moon.*

Do you have the determination to do something that's hard? Anyone can do the easy stuff. Millions of people are just walking aimlessly and sometimes mindlessly through life doing just what has to be done and even doing just what they find to be easy. Many die and the testimony of their lives may include things such as, "he was a good man" or "she was a good mother."

---

[13] www.history.nasa.gov/moondec.html
[14] ibid.
[15] Ibid.

I want people to say of me that "he had vision: that he worked hard and trusted in God to bring dreams into reality in his life." This book that you hold in your hand is fruit of that dream. Since I was in junior high school, I've dreamed about being a writer. It took me a long time to put feet on my dream, but here it is.

In the United States, many have become lazy and uninspired. Many go to their jobs, do just enough to get by, and finish the day sitting on a sofa being entertained by things that do not challenge them spiritually or intellectually. Unless they change their direction, these people will never accomplish the big stuff. Sadly, sometimes we just don't want to be bothered.

While writing this book, I've looked for inspiration and direction. For example, I heard on a podcast recently that studies show 80 percent of Americans say they dream of writing a book. However, that same study showed that only 57 percent of Americans have read a complete book in the last year.[16] 80 percent want to write a book but only 57 percent have read a book in the last year! Why? *Because it takes effort.*

I can't say that all of my years as an adult have been as productive as they should have been. I've been the couch potato before. Now I set goals for myself to keep me busy and productive. My goals for this year include reading fifty-two books, read the Bible through, and writing a book, this book! Do you think this is easy? It's not. At this point, I'm about eighteen days into my reading calendar and today I completed the reading of my fifth book. It has taken a tremendous amount of discipline. I have to turn the television off and read. I have to stay up past bedtime and read. I have to structure my time during the day to work, read, pray, have conversations with my wife and kids, eat, sleep and write; and find time for rest,

---

[16] Unknown

relaxation, and entertainment. Even though it's really cold outside right now, I am missing my favorite pastime, golf. Can I keep pace? I am determined. Determined enough to play less golf, watch less television, spend less time sleeping, etc. etc. etc. I'm making it sound like there's a price to pay, a cost to the dream. That's exactly what I'm saying. You have to pay the price of discipline. The dream will cost you other things that are important to you. A dream without a cost is not a dream at all.

Determination is a vital component to doing what you might otherwise think is impossible.

In the last chapter, I told you about my participation in athletics as a boy and teenager. I told you of my feats as a power-lifter. The end of that story is that I eventually bench-pressed four hundred pounds. Not anymore!

There's another high school story I want to tell you about. As a member of the track and field team, my part was in the field. I've never been a great runner, however, I was strong. My job was to throw the discus and shot the put.

"The shot put is a track and field event involving "putting" (throwing in a pushing motion) a heavy metal ball-the shot-as far as possible. It's common to use the term "shot put" to refer to both the shot itself and the putting (throwing) action."[17]

I remember one particular track-and-field competition during my senior year of high school. It's an individual sport and a team sport at the same time. The team gets points when its members achieve on the individual level. At this particular meet, the boy who was our one-mile runner was not able to make the trip. The coach came to me and said,

"Scurlock, I need you to run the mile for me today."

---

[17] www.enwikipedia.org/wiki/shotput

I was a 6ft tall, 225lb muscle-bound freak. I was no runner. As a matter of fact, that same year at the beginning of football camp, the coaches had all of us run the mile and we were timed. I came in at an astonishing twelve minutes. Just in case you don't know, that's horrible. Some people can *walk* a mile in twelve minutes.

My answer to the coach that day was an emphatic, "NO!"

I didn't make it a habit of telling adults "no." I was taught by my parents to always be respectful of adults and those in authority and if the answer is no, it should be framed as "No sir, I'd rather not". That day it was "NO!" The coach said, "Scurlock, I know you can't keep up with the other runners, I just need you to finish."

He just needed me to finish because there were points involved. I'd love to tell you that I did run that mile and that several minutes after all the other runners crossed the line that I fell across that same line to the cheers of onlookers. I'd love to tell you that I was determined and that my determination paid off. It didn't happen. I didn't have the determination, the gumption to try. I wasn't about to get on that track and embarrass myself.

If you are going to try and accomplish the impossible in yourself and you don't have determination, don't!

Is it easy to run in a marathon? I'm not sure; I've never done it. It sure doesn't look easy. While writing this section I decided to "Google" the question, "Is it easy to run a marathon?" The first page of responses to my query did not even mention a marathon. It was all about the "half marathon". In other words, don't be asking about a marathon until you conquer a half-marathon.

In my Google search, I found a web site that gives instructions for the beginning phases of training for a half-marathon.

"The 13.1 mile half-marathon is one of the most respected races in endurance athletics. The physiology of the half marathon is straightforward - it is a test of stamina. The keys to a successful half-marathon are:

(1) to begin with a well-structured training plan that properly incorporates your capabilities and goals and

(2) to follow that plan with unwavering consistency."[18]

Did you notice the keywords and phrases in the statement? "Test of Stamina," "A well-structured training plan" and "follow that plan with unwavering consistency?"

It doesn't' sound easy to me. It sounds like hard work, day after day, after day, after week, after month, with lots of determination. And that's running a "half-marathon", which is 13.1 miles.

The point is that people do it, not because it's easy but because it's a challenge; it takes determination! It might seem impossible at first, but you keep pressing and keep working and one day you do it. I know a few people who run half-marathons, and I'm not sure they do it with the prospect of crossing the finish line first. They do it to prove they can finish and each time hoping to improve their time! I guess it's too bad that wasn't my attitude at the track and field competition.

Determination is a vital part of faith. If faith was easy and required nothing, it wouldn't be such an important subject in the Word.

Now faith is being sure of what we hope for and certain of what we do not see. [19]

At the writing of this book I am fifty-one years old. God has put in my heart His desire to do things in my life that others think are impossible. At this point I'm not at liberty to share with you what those things are, and

---

[18] www.fleetfeetstl.com
[19] Hebrews 11:1-2

by the way, the more I pray, the more the list grows. God wants you to reach for big, impossible goals.

The enemy, Satan, will tell you every reason why you can't be used by God to accomplish difficult or impossible things.

"You're too old! You're not smart enough!" If we allow it, his voice can be a powerful force in our decision-making process. So, let's not allow it.

Peter stood in the boat with members of Jesus' team and Jesus came to them walking on the water. Peter, being the one who was bolder than the others, more vocal, and a little more brash than the other disciples, said

"Lord, if it's you, tell me to come to you." Don't ever put a challenge before God unless you mean business.

Jesus said "Come."

Can't you just hear the other disciples? They were most likely chiding Peter for listening to what apparently was an illusion. They might have been telling Peter how crazy he was and that if he stepped out of the boat, he would die. That's the kind of encouragement you get from well meaning people who have no faith.

The religious crowd is satisfied to sit in the boat and just float through life with no expectation of accomplishing the "big thing."

Peter ignored the lack of encouragement from his friends, listened to the voice of God, threw his legs over the walls of that boat, put his feet on the water and began to walk. Supernaturally the water beneath his feet became solid and he walked as though he was on dry land. Then he made a mistake. It only took seconds. He had successfully blocked out the voices of his critics in the boat but he began listening to the voice of the enemy, Satan. You've heard that voice before.

"Peter what do you think you are doing?"

"Peter, do you realize that it is impossible to walk on the water?"

"Peter, are you stupid or something?"

When the enemy started peppering him with questions of doubt and unbelief, Peter listened, lost his determination, took his eyes off of Jesus, and began to sink.

Satan does not want us walking on water. Listening to the enemy causes us to lose our determination, we lose our focus and that leads to a missed opportunity to pull off something great.

I want to say emphatically that I'm proud of Peter. Yes he listened to his fears. Yes, he took his eyes off of Jesus, but at least he tried. That's more than most people can say of themselves. I'd rather fail trying than to succeed at doing nothing.

Listen to the Word of God; "And nothing shall be impossible to you." Reject the lies of the enemy. Believe that with God, your challenge is possible and squeeze that camel through the eye of the needle.

Chapter Three

Noah

By faith, Noah built a ship in the middle of dry land. He was warned about something he couldn't see, and acted on what he was told. The result? His family was saved.[20]

The language in the Message Bible's paraphrase of this verse sounds a little simplistic. Noah was warned about something, he acted on what he was told and built a ship in the middle of dry land. What was the result? His family was saved.

Ok boys and girls. Once upon a time there was a man named Noah. God warned Noah of things that were coming and told him to build a boat.

---

[20] Hebrews 11:7 (from THE MESSAGE: The Bible in Contemporary Language Copyright 2002 by Eugene H. Peterson. All rights reserved.

Noah did what God said, his family was saved and they all lived happily ever after. It's simple. Not!

God told Noah to do something that in the context of human reasoning was impossible, unthinkable, and crazy. The writer of Hebrews account of this huge undertaking is quick and to the point. The building of the ark was not.

I'm going to stay with the Message Bible just for clarity on exactly what God told Noah to do.

"Build yourself a ship from teakwood (gopher wood, NKJV). Make rooms in it. Coat it with pitch inside and out. Make it 450 feet long, seventy-five feet wide, and forty-five feet high. Build a roof for it and put in a window eighteen inches from the top; put in a door on the side of the ship; and make three decks, lower, middle, and upper." Gen 6:14-16 [21]

I'm sure that Noah knew in advance what a huge and practically impossible situation that the building of the ark was going to be. There must have been some reservations, but in spite of them, Noah obeyed God. At about five hundred years old, Noah was most likely ready for retirement, not the construction of a ship to prepare for a flood in the middle of dry ground. Noah was a wealthy man. He had to be, in order to even begin the pulling off of this enormous task and come close to completing this assignment.

The first thing he had to do was get some drawings. You can't build a chicken coop without drawings. Actually, I'm quite sure there were no building codes or building inspectors. I'm also not quite sure how he got it done without them (sarcasm). I do think, though, that Noah had to take God's design and put it on paper. These drawings would do what all good blueprints do; tell the workers exactly how to put his boat together.

---

[21] Genesis 6:14-16 (from THE MESSAGE: The Bible in Contemporary Language Copyright 2002 by Eugene H. Paterson. All rights reserved.

So, he has his drawings. Now he's got to put his construction company together. He has to go through the daunting task of hiring workers (hundreds of them) who think he is crazy!

Let me interject right here. The logistics of this project were... well, impossible. The workers are hired and it begins. Not the building of the ship, the acquisition of materials, the main material being wood. How much wood does it take to build a wooden ship four hundred and fifty feet long, seventy-five feet wide and forty-five feet high? These are enormous exterior dimensions plus the interior walls and floors. Can you imagine how many board feet it takes to build a ship that size completely out of wood?

In the 2007 Universal Studios movie *Evan Almighty,* Steve Carrell plays Evan Baxter, a former news anchor and newly-elected congressman. Baxter's slogan for his campaign was, "Change the World." Baxter's wife advises him that since he is planning to change the world, prayer might not be a bad idea. The night before his first day at Capitol Hill as a new congressman, Baxter slips out of bed, kneels on the floor and prays. In that prayer, He asks God to help him change the world. After falling asleep reading legislation, Baxter is awakened by his alarm clock, which goes off at 6:14. Those numbers are significant because not only do they represent the numbers on an alarm clock, they represent the chapter and verse in the book of Genesis where God began giving Noah instructions for the building of the ark.

Soon after being aroused by the clock, Baxter hears the sound of a truck backing into his yard. Looking out of his bedroom window, he sees a truck unloading lumber onto his lawn. The name of the company on the truck is 1-800-Go-4-Wood. Get it? Go4wood. Say it quickly. That's right, gopher wood. That's the material that God instructed Noah to use, gopher. wood. Later in the movie, Baxter has an encounter with a man who turns out to be God, played by Morgan Freeman. Baxter is given quite the same instruction that Noah had been given. Build an Ark.[22]

My point in sharing the story about the movie is this. I'm quite sure that there were no delivery trucks dropping lumber off on Noah's lawn. That would have made things much easier. Noah and his crews had to find the trees, cut them down and then make lumber out of it and do it all without the aid of a chain saw or a lumber mill. The Industrial Revolution was still thousands of years away.

Where I live, lumber and pulpwood are king. My small town (Brewton AL) was once named one of the richest small towns in America; that wealth came primarily from lumber. For the past many years, our town has been fueled by a few major industries, two of which are a paper mill and a very large lumber mill. Log trucks are everywhere and that's good. Log trucks are a symbol of the life-blood of our community. If the log trucks ceased to roll, our community would be in trouble. The logs that ride those trucks are turned into paper and lumber.

Again, I'm quite sure there were no log trucks in Noah's community. I must repeat something I said earlier. The logistics of this project, considering the lack of technology, heavy equipment and the modern resources we enjoy in the twenty-first century were practically IMPOSSIBLE.

The Bible doesn't tell us how long it took just to get the lumber ready. I feel sure that just the gathering of the lumber took several years.

God told Noah to build an ark. It wasn't an easy task; it wasn't even just a hard thing. It was the impossible thing.

What has God put in your heart that seems so big? Do you lay in the bed at night and dream of things that seem impossible? Are you dreaming of

---

[22] Universal Pictures Copyright 2007

building a bigger ministry? Maybe you dream of starting your own business? Do you go through roller coaster rides where there are highs of faith and then the lows of discouragement and spiritual warfare?

I'm convinced of this. If God gives you an instruction or a dream, it can be done, no matter how impossible it seems in the natural.

It took Noah about one hundred years to build the ark. How much discouragement did Noah face in a hundred years? He had to endure the sarcastic railings of detractors and being the subject of jokes and laughter in the community square. Noah was no hero, nor was he a Superman. He was a righteous, godly, family man who was being obedient to God.

Can you imagine what the story of Noah would be like in today's social media world? Facebook and Twitter would be lighting up. It might look something like this: @noah must be out of his mind #building #a boat in the middle of dry ground. lol

People of this world will make light of your faith, mock your positive outlook and ridicule your dreams. Sometimes those people are your friends and even family members who are trying to protect you from potential heartbreak by trying to steer you from what they consider to be a silly dream. They think it's an impossible, outlandish dream and that "you need to forget about that, Dear, and go back to your little job." Sounds like David's brothers just before he went and kicked some giant butt.

The mentality of many is that it's better not to try than to try and be disappointed. My view is just the opposite. I've heard this statement before, "I'd rather fail at trying to accomplish something than to succeed at doing nothing." "Shoot for the stars and you just might hit the moon" is another saying that I like, but I'd like to change it a bit and say, "Shoot for the stars believing God, and you will hit the stars."

"Jeff, what if I shoot for the stars and hit nothing but miserable failure?" Shoot again! Build up your faith, read the Word, pray, trust God and shoot again and again and again!

Failure does not mean that you can't succeed. You have to just keep trying. I'll deal with the subject of failure more in depth in a later chapter.

Noah endured it all, but he kept working. He believed and the day came that the ark was completed. He finished it because he believed and trusted God. He finished it because he did not allow the fact that it was difficult to stop him.

Noah did everything just as God commanded him. The Lord then said to Noah, "Go into the ark, you and your whole family, because I have found you righteous in this generation."[23]

And Noah did all that the Lord commanded him. Noah was six hundred years old when the floodwaters came on the earth. And Noah and his sons and his wife and his sons' wives entered the ark to escape the waters of the flood. Pairs of clean and unclean animals, of birds and of all creatures that move along the ground, male and female, came to Noah and entered the ark, as God had commanded Noah. And after the seven days the floodwaters came on the earth. In the six hundredth year of Noah's life, on the seventeenth day of the second month — on that day all the springs of the great deep burst forth, and the floodgates of the heavens were opened. And rain fell on the earth forty days and forty nights. On that very day Noah and his sons, Shem, Ham and Japheth, together with his wife and the wives of his three sons, entered the ark.[24]

They entered the ark. They are saved. All the years of hard work, frustration and humiliation have paid off. Those who made a joke of Noah's

---

[23] Genesis 6:22-7:1
[24] Genesis 7:5-13

task and refused to hear a message of salvation are destroyed. Noah has been vindicated.

While we don't want our detractors to be destroyed, it does help when we feel vindicated. We love it when we can say, "I told you so." Can you see Noah shouting out of the window of the ark at those who were running for higher ground, saying, "I told you so?" I can.

It's also nice when those who were our doubters, have to admit they were wrong. If you will trust God, do what He says, and never give up, you will be vindicated. Others will see the hand of God on your life. However, in the end, it's not about vindication. It's about God getting glory out of our lives, when the camel does go through the eye of a needle.

CHAPTER FOUR

DAVID RING

I don't remember the first time I saw him. I'm thinking it was sometime in the late seventies. I do remember that he was in the pulpit at the Thomas Road Baptist Church in Lynchburg, Virginia. I was watching the television broadcast of church founder and then senior pastor, Jerry Falwell.

In the pulpit that day was a young man with a severe speech impediment preaching the gospel and giving his testimony.

A few years later, I was in our apartment in Lakeland, Florida watching the Jerry Falwell television broadcast. That particular morning, he once again had this young man with a severe speech impediment speaking in his pulpit.

I remember that morning as I watched David Ring, my emotions were impacted by this young man that said in a barely audible voice, "I'm David Ring and I have cerebral palsy; what's your problem?"

Here was a young man with his mobility and his voice crippled by cerebral palsy, and he was in the pulpit of one of our nation's most well-known churches.

I was, at the time, struggling with my own call to preach. I knew I was called, but I wasn't sure that God hadn't lost His mind. I don't mean to sound disrespectful to God. My call into the ministry didn't make sense to me. Why would God call me to preach? There were so many obstacles. The biggest one was my absolute fear of talking in front of a crowd larger than *one*. I just could not speak in front of people without breaking into a nervous deluge of sweat. My voice would tremble and crack and it would feel as though my heart had climbed into my throat. I was considering the call to preach. What was I thinking? What was God thinking? To me, it sounded as crazy as the notion of putting a camel through the eye of a needle.

Now, years later, I know what God was thinking. It was something like this: "Jeff, if you will put your trust in Me, I will do what you think is impossible." If I was going to preach, God would have to do something impossible in my life.

My wife Felicia, and I, along with our infant son, Adam, were living in Lakeland, Florida. We were located there so that I could attend school and prepare myself for the ministry. Moving to Lakeland, Florida to go to school wasn't even half the battle for me. There was more.

My fear of being in front of crowds led to a severe bout with a lack of self-confidence. Someone told me, "You don't look like a preacher." Of course, I wanted to know what a preacher looked like. Back in those days, I guess to some, preachers didn't look like muscle-bound young men that looked more like they belonged on a construction crew than in a pulpit preaching.

Going to college at the age of twenty-three with a family was an overwhelming task for me. Working a job at Kmart, and then UPS, going to school-full time, being a husband, a dad and helping with a small church; it was a load. And then there was the spiritual warfare that went on day after day; the enemy screaming in my ear all the reasons why I was stupid for thinking I could be a preacher and eventually a pastor.

Don't think Satan is going away when you declare your dream. He will attack your dream. He will do everything in his power to kill your dream. You have to have your mind made up, a resolve in your spirit and holy determination.

He came at me with all kinds of verbal attacks. "You're not smart enough! You're not handsome enough! You don't look like a preacher! You are out of your mind? Forget this nonsense; move back home and get your old job back. No one will want a pastor who has stage fright." On and on and on; it was unrelenting.

I'm sure that not everyone has the exact same battle, but I am sure that anyone who dreams the impossible dream will have battles.

I understand your struggles with believing God for the impossible. For me, being a pastor, standing behind a podium and preaching to more than three people seemed impossible.

It was during that time that I heard David Ring say, "I have cerebral palsy; what's your problem?"

As a boy and a young man, I was extremely tender-hearted. I could cry with the best of them. That morning, I cried as I watched David Ring preach with all of his limitations. Hearing him ask, "What's your problem?" tapped into a reservoir of emotions in me. As I watched him preach with his disabilities, I felt those emotions churning inside of me. I felt my eyes beginning to moisten and then it happened. The dam broke and what seemed like scalding hot tears began to run down my face. I couldn't stop them. The more I tried to wipe my eyes dry, the more the tears flowed. I'm actually experiencing those same emotions right now as I write, remembering my journey of faith, the highs and lows, and how God has proven to me that anything is possible. With the fear, insecurities and limitations that I had then, I could not really imagine that I would be where I am now. God is faithful. In my life the camel has squeezed through the eye of a needle more than once.

Here are the words from David Ring's own website that describe where he came from and where he is:

"Few individuals have felt the crushing blows that have besieged David Ring since birth. He was born to lose. On October 28th, 1953 in Jonesboro, Arkansas, David was born with Cerebral Palsy. Orphaned at age 14, he was cast about from family to family with nowhere to call home. He endured constant physical pain, humiliating public ridicule and constant discouragement. Yet, in the face of these seemingly insurmountable obstacles, David emerged not victimized…but victorious!

Life was worse than hopeless to him until his relationship began with Jesus Christ, who taught him self-respect and acceptance of his physical challenges. To most, physical challenges of this magnitude would prove to be a tombstone. For David Ring, this coming of age was and remains a milestone.

You've never heard a speaker quite like David Ring. Although difficult to understand at first, you will soon find yourself captured by his quick wit and warm personality.

Whether giving a motivational message at a sales convention, or inspiring church leaders, David always focuses on an individual's need to conquer the personal challenges and adversities of life. As you hear David Ring, you will laugh and cry. You will be amazed at his triumph over the odds. You will be moved to consider your own life. As one who has not been stifled by his physical limitations, he clearly takes his challenge to everyone. "I have Cerebral Palsy-what's your problem?" As a nationally known speaker since 1973, David shares his story with over 100,000 people each year at churches, conventions, schools and corporate events. He has been featured on numerous occasions on several nationally televised programs.

David's book, *Just As I AM*, (Moody Press, Chicago, IL) tells about his heartaches and victories, and addresses the central theme of his life; "Triumph Over Odds."[25]

My journey into the ministry started before I was exposed to David Ring, but *his* triumph over *his* odds is a great testimony and motivation for me. I want it to be for you as well.

What are the odds that you are facing in life? Is it the economy? Do you have financial problems? Marriages are failing at the rate of one out of every two in the United States. Are you about to be one of those statistics? Are you facing problems that seem to be impossible?

Maybe your finances, job and relationships are just fine but God has put a call in your heart. A dream! Has God put something in your heart to accomplish; something that you have absolutely no idea how it's going to happen? Does your dream, or your calling look impossible?

Let me remind you of the foundational scriptures for this book:

---

[25] www.davidring.com

"for assuredly, I say to you, if you have faith as a mustard seed, you will say to this mountain, 'Move from here to there,' and it will move; and nothing will be impossible for you."[26]

Jesus looked at them and said,

"With man this is impossible, but with God all things are possible."[27]

Do you have major obstacles to your dreams? Do you feel like you were "born to lose?" I want you to be encouraged. Look in the Bible at the people God used. Look around you. Many of those people who seem to be so blessed and seem to be accomplishing the impossible are just like you. They are people on a journey of faith, living a dream, and seeing the impossible come to pass.

My dream was to preach and to eventually be a senior pastor. I started out slowly. While I was attending college, Felicia, Adam and I attended a tiny church on the outskirts of Auburndale, Florida. The pastor was a man to whom I will be forever grateful. His name was Paul. Paul was a bi-vocational pastor. He was a school teacher during the day and a pastor at night and on weekends. Paul embraced and helped young men who were in college and preparing for the ministry. He also put us to work. I wasn't there long before I was up front leading worship. He also gave me many opportunities to preach. It was the ideal place. A large Sunday morning crowd might have been forty. I was given many opportunities to preach. I would stand in the pulpit, a nervous sweat pouring from my head with that same feeling like my heart was in my throat. Scared out of my mind, I would stand up there and do my best. Most of the time, my sermons didn't make much sense. After every sermon, the enemy would come with his attacks. He would tell me how stupid I looked and sounded. I wanted to quit.

---

[26] Matthew 17:20-21
[27] Matthew 19:26

However, after every sermon, my pastor would say, "Good job, Jeff" and then he would schedule me for my next opportunity.

I'll never forget the Sunday night service where it was all confirmed for me and my miracle happened. It was my turn to preach and so, as usual, I prepared. That night as I preached, I knew something was different. I wasn't nervous. There was no nervous sweat. My heart was not in my throat and the words came easier. The message was relevant and the small congregation was locked in. That night, I preached the greatest message of my young life, and I knew it was God. I knew that God had fulfilled His promise to me by performing in me what I thought was impossible.

Now, nearly thirty years later, I am more comfortable behind a podium in front of any number of people than I am anywhere else. I love preaching and teaching. What seemed like an impossibility those many years ago is now, not impossible at all. There is no crowd too large. Just give me a chance and I will stand up and boldly preach.

There have been many experiences that have fueled my journey. Many of them I have forgotten. However, I have not forgotten the words of David Ring; "I have cerebral palsy, what's your problem?"

If God can use David Ring, he can use me; and if He can use me, He can use you.

Chapter Five

Sarah

She is beautiful and married to a very rich man. Her beauty is so great that when she and her husband visit Egypt, he asks her to lie about her relationship with him. If Pharaoh decides he wants her for himself, he would first kill her husband. If Pharaoh thinks her to be only a sister, her husband is safe. What kind of woman could possess such beauty?

Her name is Sarai, which God would later change to Sarah. She is beautiful and she is the wife of an extremely wealthy man who is to be the eventual father of a nation, Abram.

Genesis 12 gives us a pretty good idea of just how beautiful she is.

When Abram comes to Egypt, the Egyptians see that she is a very beautiful woman. And when Pharaoh's officials see her, they praise her to

Pharaoh, and she is taken into his palace. He treats Abram well for her sake, and Abram is acquiring sheep and cattle, male and female donkeys, menservants and maidservants, and camels. [28]

Sarai is so beautiful that Egyptian men are taking note of her beauty; so beautiful that she is suddenly the rage of Facebook. She is so beautiful that when Pharaoh's officials see her, they praise her to Pharaoh and she is taken to his palace. This is a pretty big deal, considering the fact that Pharaoh is ruler over all the nation of Egypt. Pharaoh is powerful and can have any woman he wants. Any woman he wants! He wants Sarai!

Pharaoh eventually figured things out, after God inflicted diseases on his household because of her and she was returned to her husband.

The point I'm trying to make is that this woman had it all. She was extremely beautiful and she was married to an extravagantly rich man.

Abram had become very wealthy in livestock and in silver and gold.[29]

Beauty and money, what more could a woman ask for? Even in the western culture of the twenty-first century, that would be more than enough for most women, but not for Sarai. She wanted a son.

She is married to a man who wants a son. Not only does Abram want a son, God has already promised him that his seed (descendants) will be a great nation.

"…a son coming from your own body will be your heir." He (God) took him outside and said, "Look up at the heavens and count the stars — if indeed you can count them." Then he said to him, "So shall your offspring be."[30]

Surely Sarai knows how desperately Abram wants a son; and I feel sure that she knows about the promise that God has given him. After all

---

[28] Genesis 12:14-16
[29] Genesis 13:2
[30] Genesis 15:4-5

don't you think Abram had a conversation with Sarai that night at the supper table? "Oh by the way honey, God told me today that my seed would be such a great number that they can't be counted."

What pressure Sarai must be feeling. What extreme pressure! Here is this beautiful woman married to this rich guy who expects that he's going to have a really big family and she's not getting pregnant.

What kind of emotions was she feeling?

I have two beautiful daughters. The oldest, Kara, is married and expecting our first grandchild. The youngest, Lauren, is engaged to be married. I happen to know that Lauren and her fiancé, Trevor, have discussed children. I've heard her say that he wants as many as five.

Because I was struggling just a bit with this chapter on Sarah, I asked Lauren to give me some insight on what the emotions might be in a situation like Sarah's.

I asked her this question. "Knowing that your fiancé wants as many as five children, what would be your emotions if you found out that you were unable to have children and that adoption was not a possible alternative?" I also asked her how she thought it might affect the relationship between a husband and wife. Lauren is like me in that when answering a question, she doesn't go into lots of detail. She loves short, possibly one-word responses. She gave me several short responses that helped me with the subject of Sarai.

Lauren said that there would be "severe disappointment." In thinking about that word, I looked up the synonyms:

Saddened, disillusioned, disheartened, disenchanted.[1] Then throw in the other words Lauren gave me, depression & bitterness.

I'm not going to pretend that I have any insight into what husband/wife relationships were like in Sarai's generation. I do, however, believe that yes, indeed Sarai's issue with childbearing had to be an issue in her relationship with her husband. Did they argue because Abram didn't understand? Did she have bouts with depression thinking that Abram would be better off without her?

What a plethora of emotions Sarai must be dealing with. Not only is she dealing with those afore-mentioned emotions, certainly there's a lot of embarrassment. She's the subject of a great deal of gossip and the target of jokes.

What are the obstacles you are dealing with and what are the emotions that are a byproduct of those obstacles?

Just because I'm dealing with disappointment does not mean that God's promises have failed. It doesn't mean that there isn't a child on the way. Ok she's old. She is old and now past the age of childbearing. Her clock is ticking and the sound of that ticking is getting louder and louder.

Maybe this is you: "I'm disillusioned about my faith. I've tried and tried and I'm disheartened about the prospects of reaching a goal or having what I thought was a promise come to pass." You might declare disenchantment with faith, the Bible and even with God Himself because it seems that your promise is never going to come to pass. The clock is ticking and the sound of that ticking is getting louder and louder. It's hard to keep believing. Well friend, if it was easy, faith wouldn't be necessary.

I'm going to drop a tidbit in here that you may or may not like. Living by faith is not for wimps. Living by faith is not a life for quitters. It takes a man or woman with some guts to live by faith. I said in the last paragraph; "If it was easy, faith wouldn't be necessary." I will add to that statement. If faith was easy, everyone would be an over comer.

Why is it that some Christians seem to be happy, and others not? Why are some Christians on top of the world and others drowning in their own pity? The difference is faith or the lack of it.

Let me read between the lines just a bit. Here's Sarai going through all these emotions and the girl next door (in my imagination) gets pregnant every time her husband just looks at her. Sarai is frustrated, aggravated and mad at God. I can hear her saying something like,

"What's going on God? Why does the girl next door get all the kids and her husband doesn't even have a promise? You've got my husband all fired up. He's out there counting stars and dreaming of being the father of a nation and I can't get pregnant!"

Have you talked to God like that before? I have! I've experienced the frustration of watching my peers in the ministry flourish while it seemed that I was fighting every devil in hell just to keep my head above water.

Maybe it seems that everyone around you is being blessed and here you are holding on to a promise that seems to be getting farther and farther away.

Hold on! Don't stop praying, working and believing. Whatever you do, don't give up.

Maybe I'm crossing up the story a bit. Sarai wasn't the one with the promise. She was the vessel that God's promise to Abram was going to come through. In essence, she was taking ownership of her husband's promise. It was Abrams' promise and Sarai felt the pressure to make it happen.

Later on in our story, God comes to Abram again.

"No longer will you be called Abram; your name will be Abraham, for I have made you a father of many nations. I will make you very fruitful; I will make nations of you, and kings will come from you. I will establish my covenant as an everlasting covenant between me and you and your descendants after you for the generations to come, to be your God and the God of your descendants after you. God also said to Abraham, "As for Sarai your wife, you are no longer to call her Sarai; her name will be Sarah. I will bless her and will surely give you a son by her. I will bless her so that she will be the mother of nations; kings of peoples will come from her."[31]

In Genesis chapter eighteen God visits Abraham again. This time, however, Sarah is allowed to hear the conversation between God and Abraham.

Then the Lord said,

"I will surely return to you about this time next year, and Sarah your wife will have a son."

Now Sarah is listening at the entrance to the tent, which was behind him. Abraham and Sarah are already old and well advanced in years, and Sarah is past the age of childbearing. So Sarah laughs to herself as she is thinking.

"After I am worn out and my master is old, will I now have this pleasure?"

Then the Lord said to Abraham,

"Why did Sarah laugh and say, 'Will I really have a child, now that I am old? Is anything too hard for the Lord? I will return to you at the appointed time next year and Sarah will have a son.'"[32]

What jumps out at you at the end of the previous text? Did you skim over it or did you really read it? Go back and read it again and underline the one thing that jumps out at you the most.

---

[31] Genesis 17:5-7;15:22
[32] Genesis 18:10-14

What did you underline? The one thing that jumps out at me is God making a statement by asking a rhetorical question in verse fourteen.

"Is anything too hard for the Lord?"[33]

All through the Bible, God describes Himself with His Names. In Genesis 18:14, the name of God that is translated "Lord" is the Hebrew name "Yahweh" or "Yehovah" which means, "the self-existent."[34]

What makes God, God? It's the fact that he is self-existent; he does not require anything from any other power. There is no such thing as a self-existent human being or any other entity. So what God was saying to Abraham is, "Is there anything too hard for the only One who is self existent?" The answer to the question is NO! There is nothing too hard for God.

There are not enough words to describe the enormity of who God is and what is possible through His hand. The Holy Spirit gave us a glimpse when He inspired Isaiah to speak and write the following words, which are rhetorical questions asked by God. They are questions that are in fact declarations of God's size and power.

"Who has measured the waters in the hollow of his hand, or with the breadth of his hand marked off the heavens? Who had held the dust of the earth in a basket, or weighed the mountains on the scales and the hills in a balance? Who had understood the mind of the Lord, or instructed him as his counselor? Whom did the Lord consult to enlighten him, and who taught him the right way? Who was it that taught him knowledge or showed him the path of understanding? Surely the nations are like a drop in a bucket; they are regarded as dust on the scales; he weighs the islands as though they were fine dust."[35]

---

[33] Genesis 18:14
[34] PC Study Bible
[35] Isaiah 40:12-15

The very foundation for everything in relation to our relationship with God is found in the book of Hebrews.

And without faith it is impossible to please God, because anyone who comes to him must believe that he exists and that he rewards those who earnestly seek him.[36]

Do you believe in the God that Isaiah described? Do you believe that He exists? Do you believe that He is as big and powerful as He describes Himself to be? Do you believe that God does exist, and He is a rewarder? If you answered yes to those questions, then you are ready for a miracle.

Is there anything too hard for the Lord who is self existent and rewards those who earnestly seek Him? NO!

At the age of nearly one hundred years old, the promise becomes a reality. What seemed impossible is now a breathing human child who is born to very old parents. His name is Isaac. Now the pressure is off of Sarah. She has a son. Abraham's promise has become hers and even though she had her doubts, she believed enough to conceive in her old age.

There will be times in your life that you will think it's too late for the promise to come to pass. You will think the obstacle will be there forever, that the mountain will never move; that God is late. It certainly seems that way, some of the time. It's times like these that separate the men from the boys. Are you going to give up? Are you going to quit? It may seem to you that God is late. God may be late, in your eyes, but, He's never too late.

By faith Abraham, even though he was past age (and Sarah herself was barren) was enabled to become a father because he considered him faithful who had made the promise. And so from this one man, and he as

---

[36] Hebrews 11:6

good as dead, came descendants as numerous as the stars in the sky and as countless as the sand on the seashore.[37]

Believe God for the big, impossible thing. Don't let your challenge beat you. Ask God to put a dream in your heart and then go for it. Nothing is impossible!

---

[37] Hebrews 11:11-12

Chapter Six

Dave Roever

I think it was 1985. I was a young student pastor in Alabama and it was time for our annual state-wide youth convention. Honestly, I wasn't familiar with the guest speaker. All I knew was that I was taking two van loads of students to a youth convention. I knew that I had my hands full just keeping track of those kids and I knew that the guest speaker at the convention was a man named Dave Roever.

I don't remember the introduction but I do remember when he first walked onto the stage. I had seen some pictures and I knew this man had been severely injured in the Vietnam War. I was not totally prepared for what I saw and experienced that day.

That day, Dave Roever told us his story of being a Christian Navy Seal in Vietnam. He was assigned to riverboat duty. One particular day while patrolling the river, Dave prepared to throw a *white phosphorus* hand grenade when it was hit by a sniper bullet. The hand grenade blew up in his hand next to his face.

I could never tell Dave's story and shouldn't try. If you've never been in a setting where he tells it, you should make it a life goal to have that experience. I will tell you that when that grenade blew up, Dave lost much of his flesh, fingers, ears and much of his face.

While he spoke at the youth convention, Dave used comedy to relate his story. Yes! He used comedy to talk about having been blown to smithereens! That's what happens when God takes a life that others would throw away and performs what many would have believed was impossible.

He had a message of faith and perseverance. It was a message about love and commitment. It was also a message of patriotism. It was the Gospel of Jesus Christ. His message was funny. I laughed so hard that I cried. Before long I was crying for a different reason. His message pulled at the strings of my heart. I found myself laughing uncontrollably one moment and crying uncontrollably the next.

Here was a man who should have died in Vietnam, standing in front of hundreds of teenagers telling a story of personal triumph and he was giving the glory to God.

Before that service concluded, Dave sat at the piano and played. Not only did he play; he played well. That might not be such a big deal for someone with ten normal fingers. Dave's hands were destroyed. His fingers are not those of a pianist yet he played the piano, using fingers and knuckles. At the end, students jumped to their feet to cheer and applaud this man.

He should have died in Vietnam but he didn't. Natural wisdom says he should have quit at life. That should have been the end of dreams, goals and being an individual that God would work through. If anyone had an excuse to quit at life, it was Dave Roever. Once a handsome young man, now he is burnt beyond recognition. He had every reason to make excuses. He could have put himself in an easy chair, collected a meager living from the government and waited to die.

I would guess that Dave Roever has had his share of bad days. I would guess that he most likely experienced the same emotions that I talked about in the last chapter: disappointment, sadness, disillusionment, disenchantment and depression.

In spite of it all, Dave Roever fought back and allowed God to do the big things in his life. Today, he is a highly sought after public speaker. He speaks in churches, universities, high schools and many other venues. Additionally, Dave Roever has established the Roever Foundation. Below is a description of what the foundation is about. I share it, not to take up space. I share it because I want you to see what God can and will do in our lives when we refuse to quit; when we dare to believe Him for the big and seemingly impossible things.

The following is from the Roever Foundation Web Site:

"The Roever Foundation has a long and exciting history in support of public education, the US military, assistance to wounded warriors, and tours in military war zones, with public speaking opportunities engaging the troops with a message of hope. Additionally, the Roever Foundation has provided thousands of scholarships to students primarily in Vietnam, but also to students in secondary education seeking degrees in a variety of subjects. These include foreign students as well as domestic.

"The Roever Foundation prides itself especially in development of facilities; such as a cardiac care unit in one of Vietnam's largest hospitals, and medical teams supplying AIDS testing units for orphanages and public schools in Vietnam. The Roever Foundation built and has operated since 2000, the cardiac care unit, a Toshiba Digital Imaging Catheterization Lab, saving the lives of hundreds of Vietnamese people at no cost to them. Along with that was built a 26-bed heart monitoring system in Saigon. Cataract surgery has been provided for hundreds of Vietnamese children, giving them instantaneous vision in our 20/20 project. We have provided clothing for approximately two million children in Vietnam. The Roever Foundation has supplied extensive amounts of wheelchairs, bicycles, medicine, boats and motors to the Red Cross in Vietnam.

The Roever Foundation has continued in this effort for many years, including countries such as El Salvador and Mexico, with medical and dental support for the underprivileged.

The Roever Foundation has supported the efforts in public school assembly's tours with inspirational speaking to over seven million students in thirty years."[38]

Imagine with me, a friend of yours is in a horrible accident and is burnt beyond recognition. After recovering from the accident, your friend has horrible scars and is badly disfigured. One day your friend comes to you with an announcement. He says, "I'm going to build a worldwide ministry to students and military veterans." He goes on to say, "I'm going to speak into the lives of millions of students over the next several years." What do you think your response would have been to your friend's announcement? Be honest; do you think you would have thought it to be impossible?

---

[38] www.roeverfoundation.org

Don't feel too badly if your answer was yes. That would be the answer of the average person, even the average Christian. However, we need to turn our faith up, believe in other people and believe in ourselves. Prepare to be positive when friends and family come to you with announcements of faith. Remember the camel. With God, nothing is impossible.

What are you doing with your life? What makes me grow weary in the ministry are people who seem to have one crisis after another and they use their dilemmas for one excuse after another to never even try to effectively serve God, much less believe Him for something big. I'd love to hear them say, "Jeff, I believe God." That would be considered a victory for many.

Dave Roever is a man who, with the help of God, discovered victory and the realization of accomplishing what others thought to be impossible. Dave Roever is a prime example of what God can do with the most difficult situations. He's an example of what God can do with a willing vessel, even when that vessel is broken.

Did you lose your job? Get another one, or start a home business. Don't have a pity party. Have a get busy party. Volunteer at your church, a hospital, a nursing home or a local homeless shelter. If your life is just one pity party after another, life will pass you by. One day you will be old, life will be over and you will be full of regrets. Don't let that happen. Believe that with God all things are possible and do something.

Chapter Seven
Abraham

He waited for so many long years to have a son with the love of his life. It seemed as though it would never happen. God promised it to him and he waited.

After years of waiting for the promise, Abraham finally got the word from Sarah that he was waiting for. "Honey, I'm pregnant!" It had to be a surreal moment for Abraham. There he stood, having just received the word that what he had been waiting for was actually going to happen. What at times seemed like the hopeless dream of an old man now looked to be actually happening. Abraham, now nearly one hundred years old, was going to have his promised son.

There must have been a celebration that day. I know I'm reading between the lines again, but go with me for the narrative of my imagination.

Abraham, with his many servants and thousands of head of livestock, declared that there would be a party.

"Sarah, my wife, is pregnant, and we are going to celebrate!". He gave instructions to his personal assistant. "Quickly, go instruct the help to kill the best of the flock and prepare it for a barbecue. Gather the musicians and have them set up the stage for tonight. We will sing and dance. Put the word out into the countryside that everyone is invited to celebrate this occasion with us". The party begins as family, friends and neighbors gather at the appointed place. The music is playing and the aroma of barbecue ribs drifts through the air. The food is plentiful and the celebration is electric. The sounds can be heard in the still night air for miles around. The sounds of wild animals cannot even begin to compete with the sounds of music, laughter and joyful dancing. Abraham and Sarah sit back in their lawn chairs, hand in hand, taking in the sights.

"Sarah," Abraham said. "It doesn't get any better than this." Abraham gazes into the heavens. This special night, the stars are brighter and more plentiful than ever before. Abraham imagines what the future holds. He's sure it's a boy. There's no sonogram, no blood test, but he is certain. God promised Abraham that his seed would be great and for that to happen, it has to be a boy. He thinks about raising a son, taking him to ball games and teaching him to hunt. He attempts to count stars; something he's done scores of times as a dreamer. Now he's doing it as the expectant father. Abraham has never been happier.

Sarah has been in labor for hours. Abraham walks nervously outside of the birthing tent grimacing with every contraction as Sarah screams in pain. Friends and family wait with Abraham. Some try their hand at convincing Abraham to sit and relax while others suggest he go to the cafeteria tent for something to eat. He was not going anywhere! He has been waiting for this moment longer than he can remember. He's not about to leave Sarah; not about to miss the sounds of her labor and he surely isn't going to miss the first sounds his new son will make.

After what seems like an eternity and following what sounds like the loudest scream of the night, Abraham finally hears it: The cry of a baby!

"Did you hear him?" Abraham asks his friends who are waiting with him. "Did you hear the cries of my son Isaac?"

Someone speaks up as they attempt to prepare Abraham for the fact that it might not be a boy.

"Abraham," they said. "We are happy that your child is born. You might have a beautiful baby girl and that would be ok."

"Yes," Abraham said. "I could love a little girl, but NO! It is a boy!"

The nurse has not yet come from the birthing tent to announce the child. The only evidence that a child has even been born was the cries. Finally a nurse steps out of the tent. She has a baby wrapped warmly in soft, thick quilting of lamb's wool. The nurse is smiling as she approaches Abraham. He approaches the nurse cautiously, waiting for her announcement.

"Abraham," she says softly. "You have a son."

Years and years and then hours and hours of anticipation and waiting suddenly burst into a loud voice coming out of Abraham.

"I TOLD YOU IT WAS A BOY!"

He goes from person to person, especially those who have lovingly tried to prepare him for the possibility that it might be a girl. "I told you it was a boy!" Jumping up and down, he continues to shout, "I told you it was a boy." Abraham skips, dances and laughs deeply. His repetitive shouts of, "I told you it was a boy" are heard all around. Those around him are amused. They laugh with him and at him. They have never seen him act in such a way. He's rich and powerful. He's a man who is highly respected in the community and no one has ever seen him like this.

The nurse is finally able to get Abraham's attention.

"Abraham! Would you like to hold your son?" she asks. Suddenly, Abraham stops his dancing. The loud celebration of the moment seems to settle into deafening quiet. Abraham looks at the nurse, then at his son and says, "I've waited for so long for this moment." As he reaches out to take Isaac from the nurse, he says, "There's nothing more I'd rather do than to hold my son."

Cradled in Abraham's arms, Isaac strains to open his eyes. Even though Isaac can't yet focus and make out the details of his father's face, it seems to Abraham that Isaac is looking right at him. In spite of the fact that there are scores of family and friends standing all around Abraham, they no longer seem to be present. The only thing coming into focus is his son. Everything else fades out into a foggy blur. Their voices, once loud and clear, are now nothing but an echo from out in the distance. Abraham sees only one thing, his son. Abraham hears only one thing, his son. The man who just moments earlier had been jumping and shouting in celebration now stands rigidly still with his son in his arms. The joy of the moment begins to overwhelm him. It feels as though his heart will burst with gratitude. His eyes begin to fill with tears, and then he feels those tears, hot tears, running down his cheeks.

As Abraham looks into the face of Isaac, he remembers the conversations that he had with the Lord. He remembers the frustrations and even the stress that he and Sarah dealt with over the years. He remembers the tears of pain that came often; the long, lonely rides through the countryside and the very private conversations with God, when he dared to question His promises.

Was God a liar? Had God set Abraham up for disappointment? Was God playing sick jokes on Abraham when He instructed him to look into the sky? So many times Abraham has been tempted to not believe God. So many times he knew it would be easier to forget it, to forget the promises. It would be easier to accept reality.

Now Abraham is standing in a moment of awe, looking into the face of the son that God had promised him. Along with his feelings of awe and wonderment, Abraham also feels shame and disappointment. He had doubted the promises of God. He, at times, had decided that it would be easier to not believe God than to set himself up for disappointment.

I've been there. Have you? Have you been in that place where it seemed that God must certainly be a liar, the place where you thought it would be easier to give up? After all, the years have gone by and taken their toll; your hair has changed color or fallen out. Your skin, once smooth and silky, is now weathered with years of struggling to keep the faith. Sure you've had your ups and downs; the ups being those times that you declared your faith to God, maybe in a shout of, "God I still believe you!" The downs being those days of doubt, pain, and tears of disappointment.

God made a promise to Abraham. Did Abraham's down days and his lack of faith have any effect on the realization of the promise? I'm not sure. Would Isaac have been born sooner if Abraham's faith had been stronger? I don't know. I do know that God made Abraham a promise, and He kept it.

What will God do in your life if you believe Him? What lofty dream or seemingly insurmountable obstacle do you have? Do you believe Jesus' promise that "with God, nothing is impossible?" Read the stories of the Bible. Observe the lives of those in modern history that have overcome and achieved. Their victory came because they believed.

Please don't give up on your dreams to accomplish something big or even impossible. Your dream just might have come from a conversation with God under the stars. Don't ever give up. Don't stop counting stars.

Chapter Eight
Bill McDonald

Just a few short years ago, I didn't know who he was. I began hearing the name, but he was just another name in the long list of missionaries from our denomination who serve in other countries.

An opportunity came; I was in a meeting with other pastors. During that meeting we were all invited to travel to Ecuador on a missions trip. Up to that point, my world travels had been very limited. Felicia and I visited India in the late nineties spending thirteen days preaching in churches, colleges and even to the staff at Far Eastern Broadcasting. A few years later, I went with a group of men to Honduras to build a church. That was it. I certainly was no world traveler.

There's something powerful about going to another country, especially a developing country to be a part of the spreading of the Gospel.

Our trip to India was life-changing. I'd never seen anything like it. Little buildings packed to capacity with people sitting in the floor worshiping God and giving it real effort. They worshipped God with all their ability. That was something foreign to me when I compared their whole-hearted worship with the half-hearted worship I had grown accustomed to in our western culture.

Only one church we visited there was English-speaking. The rest spoke one of the hundreds of Indian dialects. I would watch and listen to these people singing in a language I did not understand, but I knew who they were singing to and about. It was evident that these people were in love with Jesus.

My trip to Honduras was different in that we didn't attend church services every day. We were there to build a church. We did have an opportunity to attend church on Sunday. We visited a congregation that met in an open air building where there must have been about three hundred in attendance. They sat on benches but not the padded variety that we are accustomed to in the United States. Their worship was much like that of the people in India. At one point in the service, the pastor announced that they would have their missions march and bring their missions offerings forward. I was shocked! Missions offerings? We were there to do missions work and they were collecting money to support missionaries in other countries. How cool was that?

With my limited traveling experience being all good, I jumped at the opportunity to travel to Ecuador with other pastors.

We landed in Guayaquil, the largest city in Ecuador, located on the western coast. After going through customs, it was late. We were driven to our hotel where we would bunk for the night.

Morning came and I found my way to the hotel café. The waiter poured me a small cup of coffee. After a day of travel and a poor night's sleep, it was a welcomed sight. Though I'm accustomed to drinking my coffee black, I would need to adjust this cup of 'joe' with some crème and sugar. It was a bold, South American blend. No Folgers here!

While sipping my coffee and enjoying small talk with those at my table, I noticed a new face. He was a white-haired man with a mustache and a young, smiling face. He was warm and extremely welcoming. I instantly felt comfortable around him. His name is Bill McDonald.

Bill grew up as a Roman Catholic, but accepted Christ into his life at a protestant church as a teenager. He and his girlfriend, Connie, eventually married and entered full-time ministry. After several years of ministry in the United States, Bill and Connie left the comfort of family, friends and the familiar in Louisville, Kentucky and moved to Cuenca, Ecuador to serve as missionaries.[39]

The fact that Bill left Kentucky and took his family was not the miracle (I assume). The miracle, the achieving of what seemed impossible, took place later.

It's easy to sit in the comfort of our American homes and talk about what we would do if we were missionaries. It's quite another thing to uproot your family, move to a foreign land and make that land your home; all for the sake of spreading the Gospel to those who have not heard.

Ecuador didn't roll out the red carpet for Bill McDonald. Facing rejection after rejection, Bill wrote in his book, *Change, Count on it*: "Within weeks of moving to Cuenca, I wanted to shake the dust of Cuenca, even Ecuador off my feet and go back to the safe life we had in Kentucky."[40]

---

[39] Change, Count on It. Bill McDonald
[40] ibid

The path to accomplishing the big thing, the thing that is, or looks impossible is strewn with every conceivable discouragement. When it gets really hard, that's when Satan comes with his tactics. That's when he reminds you that you should have stayed in the safety of Egypt or Kentucky or anywhere other than where you are. During those tough times, well-meaning friends and family will offer you verbal permission to give up on a dream. They will encourage you to give up. After all, what you're trying to do is impossible. You couldn't have rightfully criticized Bill had he and Connie decided to pack it in and come back to the United States. Men do it all the time. I hear missionaries talk of nervous breakdowns because of culture shock.

I've heard missionaries talk of having to return to the safety of the States because of the strain that life in a foreign country puts on a marriage. I've spoken with a missionary friend whose health was poor because of the pressure and strain of trying to spread the gospel against the onslaught of a different culture. It's not uncommon at all to receive letters from our foreign missions office that yet another missionary has decided to come home.

I'm glad that Bill's discouragement is not the end of the story. Had he quit, I never would have had the privilege of meeting him. More importantly, the miracles in Ecuador would never have taken place. Thousands upon thousands of Ecuadorian people who are now believers would still be lost, and I wouldn't' be writing this chapter in my book.

There are stories of miracle after miracle in the life of Bill McDonald, but the greatest miracle of all didn't touch the lives of only thousands, but that of many millions and maybe even more.

In 2002, Bill was given the opportunity to buy a television frequency at the price of $50,000. With no television experience, Bill raised the funds and bought the frequency. That was the beginning of Bill's journey into the world of television production. Not only did Bill raise the money to buy the frequency, he began the process of building a television ministry in Ecuador. It was a process that would have an eventual price tag of over a million dollars.

Long before Bill and Connie McDonald moved to Ecuador, God had a plan; a plan to create family friendly Christian television that would eventually reach the entire Spanish-speaking world. Though he didn't know that his destiny was television in Ecuador, Bill McDonald heard the voice of God. He and Connie heard the call of God for someone to go and they answered.

Bill answered the call and the miracles began: the opportunity to buy the television frequency, the funds to create this broadcasting power and even favor with the man who was over all cable television in Ecuador. Everything was going great until…

While in the United States, on a speaking and fund-raising trip, Bill received the call. The Unsion television station had burned to the ground; all the hard work, the prayer, the fund-raising, gone.

Things can change very quickly in life. One day you're flying high, feeling good and taking the world by storm. The next day something goes wrong and before you know what hit you, you're in a pit of despair. *Despair is the absence of hope.*

Proverbs 13:12 Hope deferred makes the heart sick,…

When you've spent all your energy seeing a dream come to pass; when everything is going so well and then without even a warning it all comes crashing down. This is the narrative of many people who were accomplishing the big thing. This is the story of men and women who have seemingly managed to get a camel through the eye of a needle just to see their triumph turn to tragedy.

This is the time that most people would understand if you just quit. It happens all the time. Pastors leave the ministry because of discouragement. Business owners decide that the dream of business ownership is not worth the fight and they close the door to that business.

When you have a dream or you manage the faith to face a challenge, Satan will do everything in his "limited" power to discourage you.

Anyone would have understood if Bill had quit. He might have even been justified doing so in his own mind. After all, he had worked so hard to build a television station. Now that station is a pile of rubble. Cameras, editing equipment, sets, lighting, everything; gone.

For Bill McDonald, the grief of the loss could only slow him down but for just so long. There was work to do. Unsion had to get back on the air; and getting back on the air is exactly what happened.

On my trip with other pastors to Ecuador, I had the opportunity to visit the new Unsion television station. It was such an awesome day, so awesome to see what God is doing through a man who dared to believe that the big thing can be done.

Today, **Unsion** television is housed in a beautiful, modern building in Cuenca, Ecuador. It's a better building, better equipment with greater vision and more potential than ever. Today, Unsion television has the potential of reaching every Spanish-speaking person in the World.

A Roman Catholic teenager, Bill McDonald, gave his heart to Christ and the rest is history. God used and is still using Bill McDonald to move mountains and do the impossible. God is using Bill and Connie McDonald to squeeze a camel through the eye of the needle.

At the one English-speaking church Felicia and I had the privilege of ministering to in India, the pastor made a statement and asked a question of his congregation. The statement:

"You have but one life to live," he said.

The Question: "What will you do with it?"

Over and over he repeated it, each time with more passion and volume than the time before.

"You have but one life to live. What will you do with it?"

Do you believe that God could use even you? If you don't, then you are saying that God cannot do the impossible. You might not have an education, charisma or good looks. You might not be a great or even a good communicator and you may think that you lack talent and ability all around. Good! Now you can quit limiting yourself because of you, and, start allowing God to do something miraculous through you because of Him!

At the time of the writing of this book, I have been in a time of prayer and fasting for a couple of weeks. As usual, I have my laundry list of things that I'm asking God for; things I'm asking Him to do. A few days ago, I felt prompted by the Holy Spirit to *ask* God what *He* wanted *me* to do, rather than *tell Him* what *I* needed *Him* to do.

You have but one life to live. What will *you* do with *yours*? What big, seemingly impossible things will you reach for? Will you be available for God to use when He calls?

Chapter Nine

Abraham, Part II

We left Abraham in chapter seven, standing in a moment of awe while holding his new son, his promise, the boy he named Isaac. Abraham had spent years having his faith tested, waiting for the promise to become flesh and blood. He passed the test. He trusted God, waited and got his promise. This, like the day Sarah gave him the news that she was pregnant, had to be a day of celebration.

With Sarah still in the birthing tent recovering from hours of labor and the intense pain that came with it, Abraham is showing off the new boy.

Girls are precious, I have two of them. There's nothing that warms the heart of a dad more than a little girl. They truly are "sugar and spice and everything nice."

I have very fond memories of having "I love you more" competitions with Lauren (my youngest). She's now twenty-one years old, but I haven't forgotten those "I love you more" conversations we would have when she was very young.

I would say something like,

"Lauren, I love you more than the whole wide world!"

She would respond,

"I love you more than the whole wide world, the moon, the stars, the sun, the mall and all the people in the mall!"

Kara, who is now married and expecting our first grandchild, would crawl up in my lap and we would sing together. Our song was "My Girl."

"I – guess – you – say, what can make me feel this way?"

I would stop singing and she would keep going with,

"My Dad!" Now she's married and "My Dad" is no longer part of the song for her.

Boys, on the other hand, are a dad's pride. You've seen the fathers at the little league game. When their son steps into the batter's box they get louder. You've seen them at the football game when their son is the one running down the side of the field, ball in hand to score a touchdown.

"That's my boy," they proclaim.

"Did you see my boy?"

"That's my son!"

Isaac grew up a normal child. He played with the other children. His dad would watch him with the other children and relish in the fact that this was *his* son and that his son was going to give him millions of descendants. Abraham and Isaac did everything together; hunting, fishing and four-wheeling or four-legging with the camels.

There is tremendous joy that comes with knowing you're in the will of God and everything is good. Abraham must have felt that joy. The test was over and he had passed. Or was it?

It must have been a surreal moment, the moment that God came to Abraham with his next test of faith.

Then God said,

"Take your son, your only son, Isaac, whom you love, and go to the region of Moriah. Sacrifice him there as a burnt offering on one of the mountains I will tell you about."

I grew up attending church. I was hearing Bible stories long before I could read. The story of Abraham and Isaac is so familiar to me that most of the time when I read this one verse, I tend to pass over it without thinking about what is really happening here.

No one knows for sure how old Isaac was when God gave Abraham these instructions. Some believe he was as young as eleven and others as old as his early twenties. Since we don't know for sure, and for the sake of imagination and drama, let's just say he was a teenager.

In order to get a grasp on a Bible story such as this one, you have to step into the story. Not literally, but with your imagination. You need to feel the heat of the desert and the cool of the shade. You need to take in the aromas and hear the sounds. You also need to ask yourself questions such as, "If I were Abraham, What would be going through my mind?" Are you there?

I'm imagining it to be early evening. Isaac is old enough to go to work with his dad. He and Abraham have spent the day riding the ranch, looking over livestock and talking to servants. Now they are home from a long day. The smell of the evening meal being prepared sweetens the air. Isaac is spending time with some friends on the banks of a nearby lake.

Abraham and Sarah are resting in the coolness of a shade. Abraham is pleased. He remembers the testing of his faith as he waited on the promise that he would have a son. He remembers the day Sarah gave him the news that she was pregnant and he will never forget the first time he held Isaac and looked into his face. Now Isaac is a teenager. Abraham hears laughter coming from Isaac and his friends. He wonders what they're talking about and he's glad that Isaac is so happy and that he has good friends. Abraham has been in deep thought and while still watching Isaac, he says to Sarah:

"You know Sarah, God has been really good to us. We have lived long lives, we are wealthy and we have this awesome son. We are blessed."
When Sarah didn't respond Abraham says:

"Sarah, did you hear what I said?" As he turns to look into her direction, she's gone. He hadn't even noticed that she had left.

"Hmmm, I didn't know I was by myself," he says to himself.

What he didn't know is that he isn't alone. I'm not sure how God spoke to Abraham that day. Was it an audible voice from heaven? Was it the inaudible voice of the Holy Spirit or did God come to Abraham in human form? Abraham had heard the voice of God in *all three ways* over his lifetime. When God told Abraham that his seed would be as numerous as the stars, He appeared to him as a man. Any way you look at it, Abraham knew what it was like to communicate with God and to have God communicate with him.

Abraham hasn't noticed that Sarah has gone inside until now. He has been in deep thought and day-dreaming while watching Isaac and his friends when he notices the stranger. The man is a stranger but looks oddly familiar. The stranger begins to have a conversation with Abraham. He makes small talk.

"So, Abraham how do you like it?"

"Excuse me", Abraham replies.

"How do you like this land I gave you?"

"Huh?" "Land YOU gave me! Buddy, you didn't give me this land, God did...." And then he knows why this stranger looks so familiar. It's Him! It's the Lord! He doesn't look exactly the same, just familiar, but the way He talks to Abraham reveals who he is. When Abraham realized that it was the Lord, he falls down on his face and begins to worship Him, not caring that anyone might see. After all, this is the Lord and everyone knows how good He has been to him.

God sits on the ground beside Abraham and they begin a conversation that sounds so normal but ends so terribly wrong.

"Abraham how about that boy I gave you; isn't he something to behold?"

"Yes Lord! He's handsome, strong and smart. I'm so proud to have him; so proud that he's my son."

Privately he's wondering why God has come. Every other time before today, God had come with exciting news. "I'm going to give you new land." "I'm going to give you a son." Abraham wondered what God was going to do for him this time. What exciting news was he about to hear?

That's how those of us in the church of the western culture think. We think we are the center of our spiritual universe and that everything is about us. We have been saturated with a prosperity message that makes it all about our health, wealth and prosperity.

Don't get me wrong. I'm all for a child of God being blessed. Abraham was! The problem is, we fail to realize that God blesses us because we put Him in the center of our universe, and His will is the number one priority of our lives.

Abraham wonders why the Lord has come to him again. "What kind of blessing will he give me this time?" He could feel the excitement building as he waited for God to spill the beans.

"Abraham," God said.

"Yes Lord."

"I want you to do something for me."

Abraham's imagination kicked into high gear.

"He wants me to do something for Him? Maybe He wants me to be even richer so that He will get more glory out of my life. "

Only seconds have gone by, but Abraham has already thought of every conceivable way that he could be doing something for God by being, healthier, richer, happier, etc.

"Abraham!" God says firmly so to snap Abraham out of deep thought.

"Yes Lord," Abraham says, but this time with his full attention on what God would say next; and then God says it.

Suddenly, it seems as though everything is spinning. Abraham is in shock. It's like the whole world is falling to pieces.

"Wait a minute," Abraham says with a nervous chuckle.

"Lord, you're going to have to excuse me. I must have gotten too much sun today. I must be delirious or something."

Abraham knows what he heard, but surely he must have misunderstood. God had given him a promise. He waited for the promise to become flesh and now God wants him to do what? Abraham continues,

"God, You're not going to believe this, but I thought You said You wanted me to kill Isaac and offer him up as a sacrifice to You."

"That's exactly what I said," God responds.

The shock and awe of the moment is surreal. In just a few moments, Abraham has gone from giddy excitement, wondering what the next blessing will be, to the realization that God has instructed him to do something horrible, something beyond imagination. Not only is Isaac his son, he is the promise that Abraham waited for. Abraham loves Isaac and can't possibly imagine life without him. *Isaac is Abraham's legacy.* As Abraham pulls himself together, he wonders if God might be about to say something like, "Gotcha!" He turns once again to look at God; He's gone.

Once again, Abraham is sitting alone. He still smells the food cooking. He looks toward the lake where Isaac and his friends are still hanging out, still laughing, still having a good time. Sarah is in the tent, servants are going about their duties like everything is normal, but it's not. Everything is not normal.

"Was it a dream? That's it!" Abraham thought, trying to make himself feel better. "I drifted off into a nap and had a dream. That's it!"

As Abraham sat in the silence of a moment, he knew. He knew it wasn't a dream. He knew he wasn't delusional. He knew he had heard from God. Did he understand? No!

That's the thing about doing something big FOR GOD. You won't always understand God's reasoning. You will not always be able to justify what you're doing to obey Him with good common sense. When you're stretching your faith to move a mountain, overcome a major obstacle or to squeeze a camel through the eye of a needle, common sense may be nowhere to be found.

He may call a young man who is timid and has extreme stage fright to preach the Gospel. That's what He did in my life. He may call that same man who is no longer as young to write a book to challenge the faith of His people. I wonder what God will tell me to do next.

Recently, I have felt very strongly that I was to make a trip to Haiti. I have an opportunity to go there with other pastors to observe the work of a mission's endeavor there. I thought that was the trip that I would take, but no. I'm supposed to "get my hands dirty." I'm not going to Haiti to preach, observe or tour. I'm going with a lifelong friend to help paint an orphanage. I don't know why. I do know that's what I'm supposed to do. Is it impossible? I'm not a great painter. That's something I usually leave to others. It's definitely not a talent, but it's not impossible. It's an open door, and I'll be doing what I feel that God wants me to do. Most of the time, that's where accomplishing the big things begins.

Abraham has heard from God; something he was accustomed to doing. He knows what he has to do. He must obey.

Abraham must have had a sleepless night. Did he tell Sarah? Did she spend the night weeping and trying to convince Abraham that he was crazy? Who knows?

Abraham began the process of obeying God quickly. Early the next morning, Abraham got up and saddled his donkey. He took with him two of his servants and his son Isaac.

When he had cut enough wood for the burnt offering, he set out for the place God had told him about.

Abraham has learned from previous experience to trust God. As hard as this assignment was, he knew God was in control and that He could be trusted.

With his donkey saddled and fire and wood in hand, Abraham and Isaac set out for the place where God told him to go. I'm sure his emotions were a rollercoaster of ups and downs; one moment, knowing that God had given him a promise and that it will all be alright; the next moment anguish, tears and the 'what-if' fears. What if it was a dream? What if I'm thinking

God will raise Isaac back from the dead and He doesn't? What if I spend the rest of my life with no heir because….?

The danger is in getting so overwhelmed with human emotions that we fail to ever obey God in the hard thing.

Years ago I picked up Oswald Chambers' devotional, *My Utmost For His Highest*. I read something I never forgot, and it fits here. Chambers said; "It's easier to serve God without a vision, easier to work for God without a call, because then you are not bothered by what God requires; common sense is your guide, veneered over with Christian sentiment. You will be more successful, more leisure hearted, if you never realize the call of God. But if once you receive a commission From Jesus Christ, the memory of what God wants will always come like a goad; you will no longer be able to work for him on a common sense basis."[41]

It would have been easier for Abraham to have ignored God's instruction. It would have been easier for Abraham if he hadn't had the call to be a father of a nation. It would have been easier to not be bothered by what God requires. According to Chambers, once you get that vision and the call; and once you decide to act on it, you will never be able to work for him on a common sense basis. Faith is not easy! Faith is not logical! Casual observers will mock your faith and the lack of common sense you are displaying. If you're going to walk by faith and do what God says, expect to walk alone; alone except for the presence of God. He's all you need.

Abraham is en route to a special place; it's the place that God had chosen. It's the place where Abraham would be taking the life of his only son. He will place him on an altar, kill him with his knife and burn him as a sacrifice to God. His mind races around in thousands of directions. In a

---

[41] Oswald Chambers, *My Utmost for His Highest*. (Westwood, NJ: Barbour and Co., 1963)

weak moment, he tries to find the common sense in what God has told him to do; but common sense is not to be found.

That's the hard thing about faith. It's hard! It's hard to have a vision for something beyond the realm of common sense. It's hard to believe God for something that can't be reasoned out in a normal conversation, but that's exactly what God wants you to do.

I just finished reading Mark Batterson's book, *Wild Goose Chase*. Batterson opens the first chapter of the book with the explanation of the title. "The Celtic Christians had a name for the Holy Spirit that always intrigued me. They called Him *An Geadh-Glas*, or "The Wild Goose." The theme of the book is the chasing of the leadership of the Holy Spirit, the will of God. In his book, Batterson reminds the reader of the "one way missionaries". One way missionaries were men and women whom God called to specific tribes. They would pack their belongings in a coffin and buy a one way ticket. They knew they would never return. Not much common sense to be found in those kind of stories, just obedience to the call of God.

This is my disclaimer: God is not going to ask you to make a human sacrifice. Did you get it? God is not calling you to make a sacrifice of anything except you. He wants you to lay your life down (in spiritual terms) for Him. God never fully intended for Abraham to kill Isaac. He just wanted to know if Abraham would be willing to lay his dreams on an altar and put God first.

God wants to know if you are obedient. He wants to know if you're available. I've often heard it said, "Your greatest ability is your availability." Amen to that! God wants you to be available. He was about to create a great nation and maybe God wanted to know that the father of that nation was absolutely sold out to Him. I'm sure God wants to know that you and I are completely His, holding nothing back. If we are, that's where miracles happen. It's the place where faith kicks into action, where the camel squeezes through the eye of the needle.

So many times we complain because we see God's hand on someone else and we wonder, "why them and not me." Consider this. maybe they have been on the donkey, headed to the mountain. Maybe they are willing to lay all their dreams on an altar and give them to God. Maybe they have declared to God that they want to please Him more than anything; more than even the realization of their dream.

Matt 6:33…..seek first his kingdom and his righteousness, and all these things will be given to you as well.

That's a novel idea in the selfish, self-centered western culture of the twenty-first century; put something or someone ahead of *"me"*. That's exactly what has to take place if you will experience miracles.

Abraham knew what it meant to put the Kingdom of God first. He did it even to the extent of being willing to offer Isaac as a sacrifice to God.

Abraham had faith in God and he was fully prepared to carry out His instructions. There is a catch. Abraham not only trusted God enough to kill Isaac, he was convinced that Isaac was God's promise to him and that, if necessary, God would bring him back from the ashes of a burnt offering and restore him back to him. After all, God had given Abraham His word and Abraham knew God would never lie.

By faith Abraham, when God tested him, offered Isaac as a sacrifice. He who had received the promises was about to sacrifice his one and only son, even though God had said to him, "It is through Isaac that your offspring will be reckoned." Abraham reasoned that God could raise the dead,….

The miracle of this story lies in several facts. First, there was a man so committed to God that he was willing to give up the most important thing in the world. Secondly, Abraham demonstrated miraculous faith on multiple levels, and third, God provided.

When they reached the place God had told him about, Abraham built an altar there and arranged the wood on it. He bound his son Isaac and laid him on the altar, on top of the wood. Then he reached out his hand and took the knife to slay his son. But the angel of the Lord called out to him from heaven,

"Abraham! Abraham!"

"Here I am," he replied.

"Do not lay a hand on the boy," he said. "Do not do anything to him."

"Now I know that you fear God, because you have not withheld from me your son, your only son."

Abraham looked up and there in a thicket he saw a ram caught by its horns. He went over and took the ram and sacrificed it as a burnt offering instead of his son. So Abraham called that place The Lord Will Provide. And to this day it is said, "On the mountain of the Lord it will be provided." [42]

He called the place "The Lord Will Provide" or "Jehovah Jireh." God has made Himself known through his Hebrew names. "Jehovah Jireh" simply means "God, our provider" or "The Lord will Provide." God definitely provided for Abraham. When God saw that Abraham was so dedicated that he was willing to sacrifice his dream; that he was willing to put his boy on an altar, that was all He needed. All God needed to know was that Abraham was totally committed to Him. When it was clear, God stopped the execution and provided a ram for the sacrifice.

---

[42] Genesis 22:14

There is another way to look at this. God is all knowing and maybe he chose to not know, to block from His knowledge what Abraham's response would be. Maybe He did know what the response would be and what He wanted was for Abraham to know. Maybe he wanted Abraham to be tested, and then grow from having passed the test.

Are you missing out? Have you missed out on the blessings of God on your life because you're holding something back from Him? Is there part of your life that does not belong to God? I can hear you saying, "Jeff, I'm saved by grace and not by works." Absolutely.Amen to that! We are saved by grace. You can't be good enough to be saved. However, you can be saved and not experience what it's like to see a camel go through the eye of a needle. You know what I mean. You can be saved, on your way to heaven and eternity in the presence of God and miss out on the miracles; the realization of the impossible in this world.

God didn't have to raise Isaac out of the ashes of a sacrifice. He could have, but He chose to honor the faith of Abraham in a different way. Abraham's seed did become like the stars in the heaven: the Jewish nation.

There is one last point I need to make about Abraham and his seed. I've heard people try and draw a line of distinction between the promises of God to Abraham and his seed in the Old Covenant and the New Testament church (me and you). What they're missing is this fact: Those stars that God showed Abraham years before Isaac was born were not just the naturally-born Jewish nation. The stars also represented believers under the New Covenant. This is why you can take any promise in the Bible and make it yours. Don't believe me?

If you belong to Christ, then you are Abraham's seed, and heirs according to the promise.[43]

---

[43] Galatians 3:29

Chapter Ten

Joseph

Jacob lived in the land where his father had stayed, the land of Canaan. This is the account of Jacob. Joseph, a young man of seventeen, was tending the flocks with his brothers, the sons of Bilhah and the sons of Zilpah, his father's wives, and he brought their father a bad report about them. Now Israel loved Joseph more than any of his other sons, because he had been born to him in his old age; and he made a richly ornamented robe for him. When his brothers saw that their father loved him more than any of them, they hated him and could not speak a kind word to him. Joseph had a dream, and when he told it to his brothers, they hated him all the more. He said to them,

"Listen to this dream I had. "We were binding sheaves of grain out in the field when suddenly my sheaf rose and stood upright, while your sheaves gathered around mine and bowed down to it."

His brothers said to him, "Do you intend to reign over us? Will you actually rule us?"

And they hated him all the more because of his dream and what he had said.[44]

It would border on crazy to write a book that deals with dreaming and accomplishing the impossible without Joseph. After all, in the Bible, Joseph is the ultimate dreamer.

There are two things about Joseph, the dreamer, that I think are important to point out. First, he was a seventeen-year-old brat. You don't need to adjust your reading glasses. That's right, in my view he was a brat and being a brat got him into lots of trouble. Secondly, Joseph did not create his dreams, they came from God. Joseph had no control in receiving them.

Why do I think he was a brat? His brothers already knew that their dad loved Joseph more than he loved them. Joseph was wearing this richly ornamented robe that his dad gave him. While his brothers were out working the farm in their sheepskin overalls, young Joseph strutted around like he knew he was something special in this expensive coat.

I have to be honest and say that I don't understand the mentality of people in other cultures. I surely don't understand what father would show that much favoritism of one child over another. One of the greatest balancing jobs of a father in the western culture of the twenty-first century is making sure that we don't show favoritism when it comes to the kids.

Mine are all grown up now, but I still have that battle. Felicia and I work very hard at Christmas time to make sure that we've spent the exact

---

[44] Genesis 37:1-8

amount of money on each child. We're so paranoid about it that we might give one of our kids like $1.23 just to balance things out. It's not really that bad but it's close. Sounds silly, but it's just that important to me that they know they are loved equally.

I love my kids and want them to know that there are no favorites. Had I been Jacob, with my mentality I would have most definitely made one of those coats for all the boys or there would have been no coats at all. So I don't understand the whole coat thing.

I also don't understand why Joseph had to prance around in that coat and then have the audacity to tell his brothers about his dream. I'm not telling you that you shouldn't tell others about your dream; of course you should, when the time is right. What I'm telling you is that if your dream interpreted means that your family will have to bow to you, KEEP YOUR MOUTH SHUT. Joseph should have known better.

The second part that I want to point out is that while Joseph might have been better off keeping his dreams to himself, he had no control over having the dreams. God gave Joseph his dreams. They were a God kind of dream.

You may be dreaming of accomplishing something really big or even impossible in your life and you'd just rather not have the dream. It's hard to dream. Do you remember the quote of Oswald Chambers that I shared earlier? "It's easier to serve God without a vision?"[45]

Maybe there are things popping up in your heart and mind that are bothersome to you. Why would God want someone to leave the comfort of their life in the United States to preach the Gospel in a third world country? Why would God ask you to do something that is financially impossible? Why would God ask you to do something so hard? *Because He has a plan.*

---

[45] Oswald Chambers, *My Utmost for His Highest*. (Westwood, NJ: Barbour and Co., 1963)

God has a plan for everything. He has a plan for you. The plan He has for you may be a small part in a much bigger picture. Remember Bill McDonald? God called him to Ecuador as a missionary. That was God's plan for Bill and it was part of a bigger plan to get the gospel to the entire Spanish-speaking world.

God had a plan for Joseph that was part of a much bigger plan. So God put the dreams in Joseph's life. Joseph must have spent lots of time dreaming of how exactly things would come into place. How would he gain so much power that his family would bow to him? Joseph might have even made a make-believe throne. Surely this was going to be fun, rising to power and seeing his older, bully brothers bow to him.

In his wildest, bratty imagination, Joseph could not have dreamed that his life would take such an awful turn.

So Joseph went after his brothers and found them near Dothan. But they saw him in the distance, and before he reached them, they plotted to kill him.

"Here comes that dreamer!" they said to each other.

"Come now, let's kill him and throw him into one of these cisterns and say that a ferocious animal devoured him. Then we'll see what comes of his dreams."

When Reuben heard this, he tried to rescue him from their hands.

"Let's not take his life," he said.

"Don't shed any blood. Throw him into this cistern here in the desert, but don't lay a hand on him."

Reuben said this to rescue him from them and take him back to his father. So when Joseph came to his brothers, they stripped him of his robe, the richly ornamented robe he was wearing, and they took him and threw him into the cistern. Now the cistern was empty; there was no water in it. [46]

I actually like the KJV or NKJV account of this story because instead of the word cistern, they use the word **PIT**. The pit was in fact a hole in the ground that was dug for the collecting of rain water. It was also called a cistern. This particular pit was dry and the perfect place for Joseph while his brothers decided what they would do with him next.

Now Joseph, the dreamer, no longer wears his richly ornamented robe. He's been stripped naked and put in a pit. He's in a place of terrible vulnerability when it comes to faith and believing for a dream, for something really big. It's in the pit that the evil one comes with his most ferocious assault. I can imagine what the voices of spiritual darkness must have said to Joseph. I've heard that voice myself. Satan must have come with attacks that sounded something like this:

"Well, hello there, dreamer boy. I guess you'll give up on that dream now. How can such a ridiculous dream come to pass? You're in a pit now, dreamer boy, just forget that stupid dream!"

The pit is a lonely place. It's dark, damp, cold and scary. It's the place where you may find yourself after you've announced your dream. It's the place where the spiritual warfare is increased. It's the place where family and friends give you uncomfortable smiles, thinking that you are surely falling flat on your face. In the pit, all seems lost. In the pit, Joseph must have doubted everything. In the pit, Joseph must have come to his senses and acknowledged to himself that he should have kept his dreams to himself.

None of it mattered. The fact that this pit was a lonely, dark, damp, cold and scary place could not change anything. Even though it was a place

---

[46] Genesis 37:17-24

of spiritual warfare, the plan of God had not changed. Regardless of the fact that in the pit all seemed lost, even this was not enough to destroy the dream. In spite of the doubts that bombarded Joseph, nothing had changed. *God still had a plan and no pit of any size was going to derail God from bringing His plan into place.* Not if Joseph continued to believe.

Don't let the dream get stolen. Don't give up on those days when it seems like everything is going in the wrong direction.

Joseph's faith must have peeked its head up at some point. It was then that Joseph mustered up the faith to believe that this pit was not his final destination. Surely he had thoughts of being rescued by his father. After all, he was Jacob's favorite. Surely Jacob would come to his rescue.

"Of course, my father will rescue me, put a new coat on me and then make my brothers bow to me in humble recognition of their wrong."

I think there came a point in time when Joseph thought he had it all figured out.

He wasn't prepared for what came next.

As they sat down to eat their meal, they looked up and saw a caravan of Ishmaelites coming from Gilead. Their camels were loaded with spices, balm and myrrh, and they were on their way to take them down to Egypt. Judah said to his brothers,

"What will we gain if we kill our brother and cover up his blood? Come, let's sell him to the Ishmaelites and not lay our hands on him; after all, he is our brother, our own flesh and blood."

His brothers agreed. So when the Midianite merchants came by, his brothers pulled Joseph up out of the cistern and sold him for twenty shekels of silver to the Ishmaelites, who took him to Egypt.[47]

---

[47] Genesis 37:25-28

What did he hear? Did Joseph hear his brother deciding to sell him to the Ishmaelites? Maybe he heard them making the deal.

"We have a slave we will sell to you for forty shekels of silver."

"Let us see," the Ishmaelite leader must have said.

After his brothers pull young Joseph up out of the pit, the Ishmaelite band burst into laughter at the sight of this scrawny little man.

"Ten shekels of silver and not one shekel more," the leader said to Joseph's brothers.

"Thirty!" Replied one of Joseph's brothers.

"Twenty, take it or leave it!"

"You've got a deal!" And with that, Joseph was no longer enjoying the luxury of being Jacob's favorite. Now he's walking behind camels, hands tied, feet bare and stepping in camel dung. It was a crushing blow. Surely the dream had been wrong. Joseph was now a slave.

Where is the dream when absolutely everything goes wrong? What do you do when no matter what you do, it comes out wrong? You go from being an individual with lofty dreams to being a slave; a slave to fear and intimidation, a slave to the disappointment of hope lost, a slave to the reality of your surroundings and you're wondering where God is. How can God allow me to go through this? Has He turned His head and looked away? Has God forgotten that we had a deal that I would follow Him if he would tell me where to go? I've held up my part. I've sung the song in church, "I'll go where you want me to go, dear Lord." I declared to my family and friends that I was following the voice of God and I was going to accomplish something important with my life. Where is the voice of God now? How can this be?

The truth is, nothing takes God by surprise. You have to say it to yourself. You have to write it on the doorpost of your heart and most of all, you have got to believe it. Don't just believe it, know it. Nothing takes God by surprise! God always has a plan, and your part in that plan is obedience, patience and faith."

Things start to improve just a bit for Joseph.

"Now Joseph had been taken down to Egypt. Potiphar, an Egyptian who was one of Pharaoh's officials, the captain of the guard, bought him from the Ishmaelites who had taken him there. The Lord was with Joseph and he prospered, and he lived in the house of his Egyptian master. When his master saw that the Lord was with him and that the Lord gave him success in everything he did, Joseph found favor in his eyes and became his attendant. Potiphar put him in charge of his household, and he entrusted to his care everything he owned. From the time he put him in charge of his household and of all that he owned, the Lord blessed the household of the Egyptian because of Joseph. The blessing of the Lord was on everything Potiphar had, both in the house and in the field. So he left in Joseph's care everything he had; with Joseph in charge, he did not concern himself with anything except the food he ate."[48]

From the pit to being a cheap slave walking behind an Ishmaelite camel train, to now being sold on the auction block to a powerful man, Joseph's life had many twists and turns. In Potiphar's house, Joseph is still a slave but now at least he's clean, well dressed and has a pretty decent job. Genesis says that "the Lord was with Joseph and he prospered."[49] Now that's beginning to sound more like it.

Yes, Joseph is still a slave but as slavery goes in Egypt, he got the 'luck of the draw' or, was it the hand of God? I don't believe in "luck." Not

---

[48] Genesis 39:1-7
[49] Genesis 39:2

in the life of a believer. No knocking on wood or rubbing a rabbit's foot. God is in control.

Could it be possible that God's plan always included a pit and slavery? God is all powerful and He could have made things fall into place much easier, but He didn't. Maybe God wanted to see Joseph's patience and determination.

Still hanging on to his dream by the tips of his fingers, Joseph must have been thinking that this job would be the stepping stone to something even better.

Everything was going pretty good until:

Now Joseph was well-built and handsome, and after a while his master's wife took notice of Joseph and said,

"Come to bed with me!"

But he refused.

"With me in charge," he told her,

"My master does not concern himself with anything in the house; everything he owns he has entrusted to my care. No one is greater in this house than I am. My master has withheld nothing from me except you, because you are his wife. How then could I do such a wicked thing and sin against God?" And though she spoke to Joseph day after day, he refused to go to bed with her or even be with her. One day he went into the house to attend to his duties, and none of the household servants was inside. She caught him by his cloak and said,

"Come to bed with me!"

But he left his cloak in her hand and ran out of the house. When she saw that he had left his cloak in her hand and had run out of the house, she called her household servants.

"Look," she said to them,

"This Hebrew has been brought to us to make sport of us!"
He came in here to sleep with me, but I screamed. When he heard me scream for help, he left his cloak beside me and ran out of the house."

She kept his cloak beside her until his master came home. Then she told him this story:

"That Hebrew slave you brought us came to me to make sport of me. But as soon as I screamed for help, he left his cloak beside me and ran out of the house." When his master heard the story his wife told him, saying, "This is how your slave treated me," he burned with anger. Joseph's master took him and put him in prison, the place where the king's prisoners were confined.[50]

Just about the time that it seems that things are getting back on track, the track breaks and there is a nasty derailment. Just about the time Joseph was prospering, he was falsely accused. Without a chance for acquittal, Joseph is thrown into jail for a crime he didn't commit. No trial, no jurisprudence and no such thing as innocent until proven guilty.

Sometimes the dream never becomes a reality simply because we are disobedient and do not follow the voice of God. Sometimes it seems that the dream will never become a reality even when, as far as we know, we've done all that God asked of us. It seems that the more we pray, believe and declare, the farther from the realization of the dream we get.

Joseph had done nothing wrong. As a matter of fact, everything Joseph did in Potiphar's house was right. He demonstrated ability, courage, loyalty and character. He was lied on and thrown into jail. Having done everything right, he was headed in the wrong direction.

There will be times when others will try and derail your goals and dreams. They will lie on you, break confidences and stir up trouble simply

---

[50] *Genesis* 39:6-20

because they don't like you and they think they have the power to hurt you. Others will misunderstand your very best efforts to do things right or judge you severely when you fail.

Joseph didn't know that the jail was all part of God's plan. He didn't know that it was all part of the plan to put him in the palace. I think Joseph would have preferred that God just do it quickly and supernaturally. I know I would. I've prayed a prayer that sounds like this; "God, I pray that you will move by Your mighty hand, and that You will do it quickly and supernaturally." Well, sometimes God does move quickly and supernaturally. Sometimes He moves slowly, but no less supernaturally. *What you think is just coincidence may very well be the hand of God working in your life.* That was the case in Joseph's life.

As the story of Joseph continues in the book of Genesis, we see the hand of God on his life there in the prison. Again he found favor. Through the interpreting of dreams, Joseph eventually had the opportunity to interpret a dream for Pharaoh. This event catapulted Joseph into the limelight, and into a position of power.

Then Pharaoh said to Joseph,

"Since God has made all this known to you, there is no one so discerning and wise as you."

"You shall be in charge of my palace, and all my people are to submit to your orders. Only with respect to the throne will I be greater than you."

So Pharaoh said to Joseph,

"I hereby put you in charge of the whole land of Egypt."

Then Pharaoh took his signet ring from his finger and put it on Joseph's finger. He dressed him in robes of fine linen and put a gold chain around his neck. He had him ride in a chariot as his second-in-command, and men shouted before him,

"Make way!"

Thus he put him in charge of the whole land of Egypt.[51]

It's been thirteen years since Joseph first dreamed the dreams. Thirteen years of ups and downs. He was challenged to stay true to his dreams. He went from being his father's favorite to being in a pit. He was sold into slavery and ultimately put in prison. Through it all, God never left him. You see it in the text. It says "And the Lord was with Joseph."

How many times have you been tempted to give up on a dream or a challenge to do something others thought impossible? How many times has your situation felt as though you were trying to put a camel through the eye of a needle? Don't quit! It took thirteen years for Joseph's dream to become a reality. Yours might come quicker. It might take longer. Either way, just keep believing.

---

[51] Genesis 41:39-42

Chapter Eleven
Deborah Ford

In the land of Uz there lived a man whose name was Job. This man was blameless and upright; he feared God and shunned evil. He had seven sons and three daughters, and he owned seven thousand sheep, three thousand camels, five hundred yoke of oxen and five hundred donkeys, and had a large number of servants. He was the greatest man among all the people of the East.[52]

Job was a powerfully rich man. According to the Job 1:3; "He was the greatest man among all the people of the East," which simply put means he was extremely wealthy and quite possibly the richest man in the world.

---
[52] Job 1:1-3

Not only was Job wealthy, he served God. He was "blameless and upright; he feared God and shunned evil. He sounds like the man I want to be. Although I'm not sure a doctrine can be formulated from Job's story, I do want to use it to make this point. *Bad things happen to good people.*

Read the book of Job. In one day he lost everything. Most importantly, he lost his children.

The question is not whether or not bad things will come. Hopefully not, but the real question is how are you going to respond when life brings you crushing blows? Sometimes getting the camel through the eye of the needle doesn't include working a miracle or accomplishing some great feat for the Kingdom. Sometimes your miracle is a testimony of survival.

Early in the morning of January 29, 1994, I received a phone call that snatched me from a sound sleep. On the other end of the line was a cacophony of sounds, confusing sounds. I could hear the sound of a male voice trying to talk to me but I also heard cries, cries of anguish, cries of "why"? I was frantically trying to clear my mind of the cobwebs of sleep. I was finally able to get my mind and ears alert enough to understand what was being said to me. The voice on the other end of the line said,

"Is this pastor Scurlock?"

"Yes," I replied.

"Pastor Scurlock, this is Lieutenant Smith (not his real name) from the city fire and rescue department. We are at the home of Richard and Deborah Ford. Their infant daughter, Kaylin, has passed away and they are asking for you."

I had only been serving that church as senior pastor for about six months. Debbie was a member there. Her husband, Richard, was a nice man but did not attend church and because I was the new pastor, I didn't know him very well. Kaylin was born with some physical issues, but had grown to be a toddler and seemed to be getting stronger. She died, we later found out, because of an undetected tumor.

I told Felicia what was going on, dressed quickly and was on my way to Richard and Debbie's home; a drive of about fifteen minutes. The entire drive, I questioned God.

"What will I say to them? How will I comfort them?"

I felt so useless, so small and insignificant; so unprepared for such a tragic event. Having been their pastor for only six months, I wasn't even sure I was qualified yet to speak into their lives.

God extended grace to me, and gave me the words to say. It was a very difficult situation. A few days later we had a funeral service for Kaylin and then moved on with life. Debbie seemed to be adjusting to things fairly well. I've heard it said that a parent who loses a child never completely stops grieving, but life goes on, even with the pain. In spite of her pain, Debbie continued to attend church and be an active part of our congregation. Time moved on and with time I felt more and more like a pastor to the people there. Debbie and her three kids became a very important part of my life. Her oldest child, Kim, became close to our son Adam, and close to our family.

As a pastor, it's frustrating to find out that families are dealing with situations but have failed to let you know so that you can be sure they receive pastoral care. On occasion, I assured our congregation that we wanted to know when they were dealing with sickness, surgeries or other problems.

About two years after Kaylin died, I received a phone call from Debbie one particular morning. She sounded happy and at rest.

"Pastor Jeff," she said,

"I just wanted you to know that Kimi is having minor surgery this morning for some female issues. I wasn't going to bother you, but I didn't want you to fuss at me later," she said with a chuckle.

She went on to say, "It's nothing serious and there's no need for you to come. We will call you when she comes out and let you know how it turns out."

After our call ended, I continued with my morning routine, with Debbie and Kimi on my mind. I couldn't shake the feeling that I ought to go and check on them. Since I was very close to the hospital I decided that I would go by for a few minutes and have prayer with Kimi and her mom.

Arriving at the hospital, I found out that Kimi was already in surgery, so I took a seat in the waiting room with Debbie and Richard. It was the typical, no big deal, feeling. We did what you do while waiting for a loved one to come out of a "minor" surgery. We talked about many subjects. As usual, the conversation moved to food. Our favorite food, our favorite restaurants, stuff like that.

All these years later, I remember our conversation about food and restaurants making me really hungry. I remember thinking that I was going to get out of there and go get lunch!

About that time, Richard and Debbie were called to the consultation room to meet with the surgeon. Having attended a lot of surgeries over the years as a pastor, these consultations can become routine. The doctor usually comes in and says something like, "everything went good, she will be in recovery for an hour and then you can see her." Because Debbie had made light of the surgery and because of the nature of the surgery, I wasn't sure if I should go with them to meet the doctor. Sometimes the family wants the pastor there with them and the doctor and sometimes not. The pastor has to feel his way through because every situation is unique.

As Debbie and Richard walked toward the consultation room, she turned around and motioned for me to come with them. She didn't seem to be concerned. She just seemed to want me to feel included. We waited in the tiny room for what seemed like eternity. It was actually about five minutes. The surgeon came in, sat in a chair across from Debbie and said,

"Kimi has cancer and there is nothing we can do for her."

He went on to say, "She will die. When she recovers from this surgery, take her home and make her comfortable."

This is a couple who, just two years earlier, lost an infant child. I'm not even sure how back-to-normal their life was after losing the first child, Kaylin. Now this doctor comes in with a matter-of-fact demeanor and tells this couple that their fourteen-year-old child is going to die. There was such a rush of emotion in that little room. It was one of those moments that, while I was glad I was a pastor, at the same moment I wished I wasn't. It was one of those moments that my heart was breaking for the parents and at the same time, I felt the weight of the world because I was supposed to say something spiritual and profound. The right words were at a premium. All I knew to do was to wrap my arms around this mom and dad and tell them I was sorry. Not much faith in the phrase, "I'm sorry." Honestly, that was all I could come up with.

A few days later, Kimi was flown from Crestview, Florida to Shands Hospital in Gainesville, Florida. There, she was going to see a specialist for an evaluation and prognosis. We were praying and believing for a miracle, but we also put hope in this new doctor. Hopefully he would see it differently than the surgeon. Hopefully he would tell Debbie and Richard that he could help Kimi. That's not what happened.

The new doctor's prognosis was the same as the surgeon's. He told the parents that there was nothing he could do and because Kimi had not yet been told, it was time to tell her how sick she was. He wanted to go to her room at that moment and tell her, but Debbie said, "Not before our pastor gets here."

I received the news from Debbie and the request that I come immediately. I threw a few things together, put my car on Interstate 10 and pointed it toward Gainesville, a five hour drive. Five hours to pray. Five hours to think. I wondered how Kimi was going to respond and what I would say. It was a long, lonely five hours.

I found Kimi in an ICU bed with her parents and grandparents around her. The doctor and his nurse arrived for this dreadful meeting. We were asked to step into the hall for the doctor's instructions that we were to show no emotion as he talked with Kim. My thought, "That's easier said than done pal."

When we entered the room, Kimi knew something was up, but she wasn't prepared for what she was about to hear. The family stood next to the bed on her left side. The doctor sat on the bed on the right side. Behind him were his nurse and me. The doctor leaned over Kimi, putting his arm across her body and bracing himself with his hand on the other side. He was very calm and warm. He put his face close to Kimi's and looking directly into her eyes said,

"Kim, you're very sick and there is nothing I can do for you."

A few moments passed. I watched Kimi closely, but also shot my eyes toward her parents to monitor their well-being. Her mom looked as though she was about to explode but trying with all her might to honor the doctor's instructions. She managed to keep her emotions at bay. I watched

Kimi. It was only a few seconds but seemed longer. She wasn't sure what the doctor was saying. He asked her,

"Kim, do you understand what I'm saying to you? You're a very sick young lady and I can't cure you."

Then it became clear to her. I was looking right at her when the realization of what the doctor was telling her hit home. Suddenly her face transformed from quiet and peaceful to horrified. Kimi began to look at each person who stood around her bed. Looking for someone to reassure her, there was no reassurance to be found. I felt as though I had a volcano trying to erupt inside of me. My body convulsed as I held back the emotions that were exploding inside of me. I looked at Debbie, Richard and the grandparents. They were beginning to lose the battle of containing emotions. It was the worst moment of Debbie's and Richard's life. It was the worst day of my life, too.

Having delivered the news, the doctor stepped away from the bed and exited the room. I stepped up to the bed to be the spiritual giant I was supposed to be. Kimi looked at me and said,

"Pastor Jeff, you have to promise me that I'm not going to die."

Seventeen months later, I drove to the Crestview Hospital because I received word that it wouldn't be long. It was very late.

I had been in a Bible study at the church before being called to the hospital. The hospital corridors were empty. There were no visitors at this hour. When I stepped into Kimi's room, the lights were low and it was quiet; quiet except for the low sobs of a few teenage girls who were there. Debbie stood next to the bed. I had been at the deathbed of people several times before. I knew the signs. The time between breaths was getting longer and longer. I knew that Kimi was about to leave this world. Her mom ran her fingers through what hair Kim had left and cried. *Her baby, her second baby in two years*, was about to step to the other side.

I leaned over, put my mouth to Kim's ear and said.

"Kimi, I'm so jealous. Your about to see Jesus, and it's going to be awesome."

Just a few weeks earlier, I had been summoned to the hospital in Pensacola, Florida by Kimi. She wanted to talk about death.

"Pastor Jeff, what is it like to die?"

"I'm not sure," I responded.

I told her, "The Bible says that death has no sting for a Christian."

"What does that mean?" she asked.

"Kimi," I said. "I think when we die, we step from this world into that world and it doesn't hurt and it's not scary."

"I was afraid I would be scared," she said. "I've never been on any long trips without my mom and I don't want to leave her."

I tried to reassure her:

"Time is different in heaven," I said. "I believe that when you get there, your mom will be right behind you." You won't be alone or lonely, Heaven is a wonderful place."

My attempt to reassure her seemed to work. She seemed peaceful when I left her that day.

Now she's about to make that journey.

I know what someone is thinking right now.

"Jeff, if you had any faith, you would have rebuked that cancer and she would have been healed." I don't know. I wrestle with my faith at times. I've seen people healed of cancer. I don't have all the answers. All I know is that I believe the Word. Hopefully, the blanks will be filled in when I get to heaven and I will understand more. There's an old, old song that says, "Farther along we'll will know all about it. Farther along we'll understand why. Cheer up, my brother, live in the sunshine. We'll understand it all by and by."[53]

There we all were, Kimi, her family, some of her friends, her pastor and a nurse. We held hands and prayed. There were tears all around. We began to sing Amazing Grace. I'm not sure who started it, but everyone, including the teenage girls and the nurse sang. Just a few moments later, Kimi took her last breath.

Other than the fact that the 350 seat auditorium was standing room only, I don't remember much about the funeral. It was a very painful time for many people.

I've told this whole story to get to this point and say this. If anyone had a reason to be bitter, it was Deborah. If anyone could be justified (in the natural) in deciding not to worship God, it was Deborah.

I get so weary with people who can't keep the faith when they're going through little things. They get bitter because they struggle financially. They quit attending church because someone hurt their feelings. I've had people in my life in the ministry who couldn't say a positive thing or demonstrate faith if their life depended on it. It's all gloom and doom, one crisis after another. Compared to Debbie, they don't have a crisis.

This is the place where I'm supposed to tell you that Debbie quit attending church because she was bitter. Or I'm supposed to tell you that Debbie had to be put in a mental hospital because of a nervous breakdown.

I can't tell you those things because they wouldn't be true. The truth is this. In the three or so years that I remained as pastor of that church, I never heard one word of bitterness out of Debbie. I could count on Debbie

---

[53] Farther Along, W.B. Stevens 1911

to be in her seat on Sunday mornings. It was always the second row on the center aisle.

Some individuals sit through the worship services and absolutely refuse to worship. Not Debbie! She was on her feet, hands raised in worship. There were usually tears and I'm quite sure that most of the time those tears were there because of pain. In spite of it, Debbie worshiped. Debbie worshiped through the pain.

What is the miracle in this story? *The miracle is survival.* What was accomplished that someone might think is impossible? Faith and survival.

Ten years after Kimi went to heaven, Richard and Debbie buried a third child. Their teenage son, Dakota, died from cancer in 2008. That's right. Richard and Debbie Ford have buried three of their four children.

When I decided that I would tell this story, I visited Debbie's Facebook page. There I found her favorite quote. It comes from the Bible, "I can do all things through Christ who strengthens me."[54]

Today, Debbie continues to be a committed Christian who is faithful to her relationship with God and her church. She is a testimony of survival. She is an example to all of us who think we can't go forward or have any hope. She is a modern-day woman who has gone through hell trying to get a camel through the eye of a needle and succeeded.

She did get her camel through the eye of her needle. I'm sure Debbie can't say for sure how she survived, except for the fact that she trusted God and He has performed the impossible in her life.

If you're going through something really difficult, remember this: God is going through it with you. Consider the fact that it might be hard right now because the camel is stuck, but keep pushing, keep believing, keep

---

[54] Philippians 4:13

trusting in God. He is faithful and will not leave you. Keep putting your faith in what you know God's Word says. Believe and never give up.

Chapter Twelve
Paul and Silas

His name is Saul. He is an educated, religious zealot who is making it his mission to stop this new movement of people who are following the teachings of Jesus. After all, as far as Saul knows, Jesus had been executed on a cross. Yes, there was an empty tomb, but Saul and those like him are convinced that Jesus' body had been stolen by His followers. The frustrating part is that in spite of all their financial backing, manpower and effort, they have not been able to find that body.

Frustrations are growing because of the multiplying rumors that Jesus has been seen alive since the execution. Now there is a growing movement and things are getting out of hand. There are thousands who joined the movement on Pentecost and news of such conversions are coming in daily.

Saul is present at the first stoning of one of the members of this new movement. He watched with great pride and satisfaction as Stephen was stoned.[55]

Saul has heard of a growing movement in Damascus and he is not about to stand idly by and let it go unchallenged. So Saul goes to the High Priest and gets authority to arrest and persecute these followers of Jesus.

Meanwhile, Saul was still breathing out murderous threats against the Lord's disciples. He went to the high priest and asked him for letters to the synagogues in Damascus, so that if he found any there who belonged to the Way, whether men or women, he might take them as prisoners to Jerusalem.[56]

Saul was determined to do his part and if that meant going to Damascus, that's what he would do. He loaded up, recruited some help and headed out for the little town. He was in for a surprise and for an event that would change his life and the church for all eternity.

As he neared Damascus on his journey, suddenly a light from heaven flashed around him. He fell to the ground and heard a voice say to him,

"Saul, Saul, why do you persecute me?"

"Who are you, Lord?" Saul asked.

"I am Jesus, whom you are persecuting," he replied.

"Now get up and go into the city, and you will be told what you must do."[57]

"I am Jesus, whom you are persecuting." Wow! What in the world is going through Saul's mind now? He has been blinded by a light and hears a voice of someone who identifies himself as Jesus; the same Jesus whose

---

[55] Acts 7:58
[56] Acts 9:1-2
[57] Acts 9:3-6

disciples he has been persecuting, arresting and even participating in their execution; the same Jesus whose movement he is planning to silence in Damascus; the same Jesus who Saul believed was dead. He would never be the same.

I need to make this point before I move on with the story. Lots of people need a real encounter with Jesus. We have people sitting in the seats of our churches who have never had an exchange with Jesus, never confessed him as Lord and subsequently have never become born again. They come to church and we call them "brother", but their hearts are still dark because of the absence of that most important encounter.

You probably won't be blinded by a light when you have this encounter. You most likely won't hear voices but you will have a life-changing experience when you become a disciple of Jesus.

It happened to Saul. His life was changed forever. Let's continue with the scripture.

The men traveling with Saul stood there speechless; they heard the sound but did not see anyone. Saul got up from the ground, but when he opened his eyes he could see nothing. So they led him by the hand into Damascus. For three days he was blind, and did not eat or drink anything. In Damascus there was a disciple named Ananias. The Lord called to him in a vision,

"Ananias!"

"Yes, Lord," he answered.

The Lord told him,

"Go to the house of Judas on Straight Street and ask for a man from Tarsus named Saul, for he is praying. In a vision he has seen a man named Ananias come and place his hands on him to restore his sight."

"Lord," Ananias answered, "I have heard many reports about this man and all the harm he has done to your saints in Jerusalem. And he has come here with authority from the chief priests to arrest all who call on your name."

But the Lord said to Ananias, "Go! This man is my chosen instrument to carry my name before the Gentiles and their kings and before the people of Israel. I will show him how much he must suffer for my name."

Then Ananias went to the house and entered it. Placing his hands on Saul, he said, "Brother Saul, the Lord Jesus, who appeared to you on the road as you were coming here — has sent me so that you may see again and be filled with the Holy Spirit." Immediately, something like scales fell from Saul's eyes, and he could see again.

He got up and was baptized, and after taking some food, he regained his strength.[58]

From that day forward, Saul is no longer persecuting Christians – *he has actually become one of them.* He almost immediately begins preaching the gospel.

Somewhere along the way, he became known as Paul. He was Saul who was also Paul.

Paul becomes the greatest missionary/evangelist of the New Testament church. His life is spent doing missionary work, and serving lots of time in jail. Now he is not persecuting believers, he's one of the persecuted.

On one of his missionary journeys, Paul teams up with a man named Silas. We don't know that much about Silas other than the fact that he is on

---

[58] Acts 9:7-19

this trip with Paul. In the city of Philippi, Paul and Silas encounter a slave girl who is a demon-possessed fortune teller.

Once when we were going to the place of prayer, we were met by a slave girl who had a spirit by which she predicted the future. She earned a great deal of money for her owners by fortune-telling. This girl followed Paul and the rest of us, shouting,

"These men are servants of the Most High God, who are telling you the way to be saved."

She kept this up for many days. Finally Paul became so troubled that he turned around and said to the spirit,

"In the name of Jesus Christ I command you to come out of her!" At that moment the spirit left her.[59]

It was one of those days when trying to do what was right turned out so wrong.

Have you been there? Have you been in a situation where all you did was what you believed to be the right thing, and your day, your week, your month and maybe even your life was turned upside down? Paul and Silas are having one of those days.

This girl has been pestering Paul and Silas for days and they have had just about enough of it. Paul swings around toward the girl, who was following them, pulls his spiritual authority out and casts the devil out of her. Instantly she is set free. Free from the spiritual darkness that has tormented her for so long. Free from the misery of a dark, demon-controlled life. There is only one problem. She can no longer predict the future. That's a problem because she is a slave girl and her ability to predict the future has been a source of income for her owners.

---

[59] Acts 16:16-18

When the owners of the slave girl realized that their hope of making money was gone, they seized Paul and Silas and dragged them into the marketplace to face the authorities. They brought them before the magistrates and said,

"These men are Jews, and are throwing our city into an uproar by advocating customs unlawful for us Romans to accept or practice."

The crowd joined in the attack against Paul and Silas, and the magistrates ordered them to be stripped and beaten. After they had been severely flogged, they were thrown into prison, and the jailer was commanded to guard them carefully. Upon receiving such orders, he put them in the inner cell and fastened their feet in the stocks.[60]

Paul and Silas are attacked, dragged to the town square to face the authorities and then lied on. Because of the lie, they are stripped naked (in public) and beaten. After being severely beaten they are thrown into prison. All in all, their day has not turned out like they planned. All they wanted to do was to tell people about Jesus and make converts of those who would listen. They were on a good mission.

Their good mission has landed them in jail. Put into the inner prison, Paul and Silas are sitting with their feet in stocks. The severe beating they have experienced has left them racked with pain. They're sitting in pools of their own blood, mixed with dried human feces left behind by other prisoners. The conditions of the inner prison are deplorable. Very little light is trickling in. The smell was sickening. It smelled of human feces, urine, body order, dried blood and who knows what else. This was the worst place Paul and Silas could have ended up. No human being should have to experience such an awful place.

---

[60] Acts 16:19-24

As darkness falls, what natural light that may have been present is fading away. Now the only light is a lantern the jail keeper has in his quarters. There's barely enough light to see much of anything or anyone. With darkness comes hopelessness for the prisoners.

Some go to sleep. Others are moaning in pain from beatings similar to what Paul and Silas have experienced today. You can even hear the sounds of quiet crying coming from men who are hopeless and weep at the memory of a better time.

Paul and Silas, too, suffer from pain, humiliation and the temptation to give up hope. Would they die in this prison? Is this how it would end? Not long ago, Paul sat at the table with the most important men in the Jewish society. He wore the best clothes and ran in the best circles. He was an up and coming young man with a promising future. Now he's naked, dirty, injured and in the worst of all possible places.

The hour grows later and later. With every passing hour, hope seems to diminish more and more. Any attempt to be positive in such conditions gets harder with each passing moment.

Whatever it is that you might be dealing with, there will be temptation to give up and lose hope. There will be those who will encourage you to hang in there and others who will encourage you to give up.

If God has put a dream, a vision, or the call to do something others think is impossible in your heart, quitting cannot be an option.

Midnight is approaching. Paul and Silas are extremely uncomfortable in their surroundings and have found it impossible to sleep. Have you ever noticed how everything seems worse late at night or in the wee hours of the morning? That earache always gets worse at night. A feeling of hopelessness grows stronger in the night. The fever returns in the night.

Paul and Silas feel the chill of the night air in their dark and damp accommodations. What would the rest of the night bring? What would the next day bring? They didn't know. They did know, however, that they were on a mission; a mission for God and there was something that was uniquely special about suffering for the Kingdom of God. Strangely enough, this suffering brings joy. In a situation where many believers would crumble, Paul and Silas found joy in their sufferings. In a situation where many believers would grumble and complain, Paul and Silas decided to worship their God.

About midnight Paul and Silas were praying and singing hymns to God, and the other prisoners were listening to them. [61]

At a moment when most would crumble beneath the pressure, Paul and Silas are worshipping God. They are singing songs of praise and worship and giving glory to God!

The enemy's goal is to shut up your praise, to shut your witness up, to stop you from saying one more good thing about your God. That's what he wanted to do to Paul and Silas, but they refused.

In the worst possible conditions, they are praising God. No band, no stage lighting, no worship leader. Just an intense love and trust in Jesus.

We, in western civilization, need to rediscover our passion for the King who has set us free. We need to make sure there is a fire burning in our hearts for the things of God, and if not, we need to allow Him to reignite those fires.

The miracle of Paul and Silas was their faith. It was their worship in difficult times. It was the determination and resolve that no matter what, they would worship God.

---

[61] Acts 16:25

If you are facing a camel that needs to go through the eye of a needle, worship God. Worship is more valuable, more effective and I believe it means more to God when it comes out of pain or a difficult time.

Paul spent most of his life after his conversion in prison, but his life meant so much. So much that two thousand years later, his relationship with Jesus and his commitment to the gospel is impacting souls worldwide in the twenty-first century.

Where does your relationship with Jesus stand? How about your commitment to the gospel? Are you willing to lay your life down for Jesus? Are you willing to do what it takes to spread the good news that Jesus saves?

It's time to use our faith. It's time to resurrect old faith that we have allowed to die. It's time to believe once again that even though it is impossible with men, that with God, all things are possible.

When Paul and Silas began praising God, the prison bars were opened, but in my mind that's not the miracle. The miracle came when Paul and Silas sang and worshipped in the worst of times.

Are you a worshipper or a whiner? Are you a believer or a doubter? Are you going to get your camel through the eye of your needle or will you just let life pass you by and refuse to believe God for anything?

So times are tough, Suck it up! Stretch your faith; worship God in spite of your troubles. Who knows? The bars may just fly open for you too.

Chapter Thirteen
Shadrach, Meshach and Abednego

It's not their real names given to them by their mother. They were Israeli boys, part of the tribe of Judah. Jerusalem has been attacked by Nebuchadnezzar king of Babylon and taken captive.

They are very handsome, intelligent and gifted young men. I'm sharing this account with you from the book of Daniel so that you can see the quality of these guys, their real given names and the point where their names were changed.

Then the king (Nebuchadnezzar) ordered Ashpenaz, chief of his court officials, to bring in some of the Israelites from the royal family and the nobility— young men without any physical defect, handsome, showing aptitude for every kind of learning, well informed, quick to understand, and qualified to serve in the king's palace. He was to teach them the language and literature of the Babylonians. The king assigned them a daily amount of food and wine from the king's table. They were to be trained for three years, and after that they were to enter the king's service. Among these were some from Judah: Daniel, Hananiah, Mishael and Azariah. The chief official gave them new names: to Daniel, the name Belteshazzar; to Hananiah, Shadrach; to Mishael, Meshach; and to Azariah, Abednego. [62]

Moreover, at Daniel's request the king appointed Shadrach, Meshach and Abednego administrators over the province of Babylon, while Daniel himself remained at the royal court.[63]

I know you get the point after reading these scriptures. Shadrach, Meshach and Abednego, are sharp and talented men. They are Jews, captive in Babylon but have been given much authority because of their abilities.

As you know, they are also very faithful to God. Later in this book, I will be discussing Peter and failure; how God's grace restored Peter in spite of his failure. This story is a polar opposite to the story about Peter. These are guys that are going to stand for God, even to the point of death if necessary, and nothing is going to cause them to back down. The point of this chapter is that just as failure will put you in an impossible situation, doing what is right will, too. Don't think that because you have solid morals, high spiritual standards and that you always do your very best to do what's right, that you will always be celebrated. Don't think you won't be faced with a big fat camel and a tiny needle.

These three Israeli men are righteous, smart, upstanding citizens and they are true to their God, and for all that goodness, they are not rewarded (initially) with good but with bad.

---

[62] Daniel 1:3-7
[63] Daniel 2:49

The action begins in the story when King Nebuchadnezzar made an image that was ninety feet tall for everyone under his rule to worship.

King Nebuchadnezzar made an image of gold, ninety feet high and nine feet wide, and set it up on the plain of Dura in the province of Babylon. He then summoned the satraps, prefects, governors, advisers, treasurers, judges, magistrates and all the other provincial officials to come to the dedication of the image he had set up. So the satraps, prefects, governors, advisers, treasurers, judges, magistrates and all the other provincial officials assembled for the dedication of the image that King Nebuchadnezzar had set up, and they stood before it. Then the herald loudly proclaimed, "This is what you are commanded to do, O peoples, nations and men of every language: As soon as you hear the sound of the horn, flute, zither, lyre, harp, pipes and all kinds of music, you must fall down and worship the image of gold that King Nebuchadnezzar has set up. Whoever does not fall down and worship will immediately be thrown into a blazing furnace."[64]

This decree should have put every Jew present into a very awkward position, considering that the Law of Moses said, "You shall have no other Gods before Me."[65]

"Surely," Shadrach said, "Every Jew will rebel against this order."

Surely they don't. There is no record in the Bible of anyone who refused to bow other than Shadrach, Meshach and Abednego. These three Hebrew men decide they will not bow.

Think of the rationale of that decision and the justification and reasoning they could come to. "Everyone else is bowing, so God would understand if we bow just this one time." They could have easily

---

[64] Daniel 3:1-6
[65] Exodus 20:3; Deuteronomy 6:7

succumbed to peer pressure. After all, no one wants to be thrown into a fiery furnace.

The mindset of many people in the twenty-first century who claim to be followers of Christ is full of excuses like: "Everyone else is doing it, so surely it would be ok with God if I do it, too."

I believe with all my heart that we are saved by grace and not works. As a matter of fact, one of my favorite Bible passages declares it.

Therefore, there is now no condemnation for those who are in Christ Jesus, because through Christ Jesus the law of the Spirit of life set me free from the law of sin and death.[66]

We are free from the law of sin and death and are alive through the Spirit of life in Christ Jesus. I believe that. I preach it. It's the theme of my life. Thank God for His grace. Keep in mind other things Paul says about grace.

What then? Shall we sin because we are not under law but under grace? By no means! Don't you know that when you offer yourselves to someone to obey him as slaves, you are slaves to the one whom you obey — whether you are slaves to sin, which leads to death, or to obedience, which leads to righteousness?[67]

What does it mean? It means that we don't bow to the idols of this world just because we have grace. We say "no" to sin. We, as believers, are charged to do what is right EVERY TIME. If not, according to Paul, we become slaves to sin, and being a slave to sin, leads to death. In other words, a lifestyle of constantly choosing the wrong path will ultimately separate you from God and lead to death.

Grace is not permission to sin; it's the motivation for living right!

---

[66] Romans 8:1-2
[67] Romans 6:15-16

Again let me say it. When faced with a decision between right and wrong, we should always decide to do what is right in God's eyes. Right morals, right spiritual decisions, right in business affairs, right in marital relationship, etc., etc., etc.

According to what I read in Daniel, of all the thousands who were in captivity, only three chose not to bow. It's possible that others refused too, and that the Bible doesn't have record of them, but it would appear that everyone else played it safe and did the wrong thing.

In spite of, or because of their positions of authority, Shadrach, Meshach and Abednego's decision not to bow infuriated Nebuchadnezzar. They were embarrassing him.

Furious with rage, Nebuchadnezzar summoned Shadrach, Meshach and Abednego. So these men are brought before the king, and Nebuchadnezzar said to them,

"Is it true, Shadrach, Meshach and Abednego, that you do not serve my gods or worship the image of gold I have set up? Now when you hear the sound of the horn, flute, zither, lyre, harp, pipes and all kinds of music, if you are ready to fall down and worship the image I made, very good. But if you do not worship it, you will be thrown immediately into a blazing furnace. Then what god will be able to rescue you from my hand?"[68]

I think Nebuchadnezzar really likes these boys. They are talented, smart and part of his leadership team. I think he is so furious because he is embarrassed that some of his own guys are refusing to bow, so he decides to give them another chance.

"What a relief," these boys must have thought.

"We made a really bad decision the first time not bowing with everyone else, but Nebuchadnezzar is going to give us a do-over. Wow!

---

[68] Daniel 3:13-15

Thanks King Neb. You don't know how much we appreciate a second chance. You know it's hot out here and the sun must have gotten to our brains. We don't know what we were thinking!"

"Strike up the band O King. Just as soon as we hear that music, we will bow." **NOT!**

That's not what they said at all! These boys are faced with a real 'camel, eye of the needle' challenge. Here they stand before the king. They feel the heat from the furnace which makes the heat of the moment more intense and they have to decide if they are going to accept Nebuchadnezzar's offer of grace and bow, or will they refuse again and meet their end in the furnace.

There will be times in life that you will feel the heat. There will be decisions that will affect your character, your morals, who you are as a human and who you are as a believer. No one has ever said that it's always easy to do the right thing. I wish I could say that I've always done it right. I've made bad decisions. I, like many of you, have wept the same kind of tears that Peter did after he denied Jesus. I have experienced regret because of bad decisions. We are all faced with very important decisions almost on a daily basis.

Years ago, before I entered full-time ministry, I worked a job in the oil field industry. One day, I used a roll of electrical tape on the job. I still had it in my pocket when my shift was over and it was time to go home. I remembered that I had a little project at home and that I needed some electrical tape. I made a quick decision. "No one will miss this electrical tape. This job I'm on is going to make this company hundreds of thousands of dollars. Surely one little roll of electrical tape won't matter. I took the tape with me. The entire one and a half hour drive home I wrestled with guilt and conviction. What I had done was steal, and stealing is wrong. I struggled with my conscience and most likely the Holy Spirit, too. It was wrong for me to take that roll of tape away from the job for my personal use.

"But Lord, it's just a little roll of tape," I argued.

Nevertheless, it was stealing. Was it any less wrong than if I had taken something of great value? No.

I was so happy to get back to work the next day and put that tape back where it belonged without having used it at home. You may think that's a silly example, but it's no laughing matter with God.

We live in difficult financial times. The prosperity our nation has known over the last couple of decades has gone away and our economy has slipped into deep recession. More and more, we hear stories of the powerfully rich who are going to prison because of bad financial decisions; decisions to do whatever it takes to keep their head above water to make some extra money. Even the blue collar 'Joe the plumber' types are faced with decisions of character.

I have faced challenges and tests over the years that were bigger than a roll of tape, but God has never allowed me to forget the tape. It means something to Him when we make right decisions. Doing the right thing may put you into a seemingly impossible course of events, but I'm convinced that God will honor and bless you when you do the right thing.

Shadrach, Meshach and Abednego decide to do the right thing, even though it's the hardest thing they had ever done in their lives.

Shadrach, Meshach and Abednego replied to the king,

"O Nebuchadnezzar, we do not need to defend ourselves before you in this matter. If we are thrown into the blazing furnace, the God we serve is able to save us from it, and he will rescue us from your hand, O king. But even if he does not, we want you to know, O king, that we will not serve your gods or worship the image of gold you have set up."[69]

Can you hear the murmuring of those who stood nearby as they whispered among themselves concerning the decision that these young men are making?

"Are they stupid or something?"

There are no text messages, no tweets and no Facebook updates. Fox News isn't there to immediately broadcast the news worldwide via satellite, but you can rest assured that the news is traveling fast, person to person; the news that Shadrach, Meshach and Abednego are still refusing to bow. Now Neb is really angry.

"These boys have the audacity to make this stand and embarrass me in front of all Babylon." Nebuchadnezzar is angry.

Now he couldn't care less who they are, and he has no intention of giving them yet a third opportunity to bow.

Now Nebuchadnezzar is furious with Shadrach, Meshach and Abednego, and his attitude toward them has changed. He orders the furnace heated seven times hotter than usual and commands that some of the strongest soldiers in his army tie up Shadrach, Meshach and Abednego and throw them into the blazing furnace. So these men, wearing their robes, trousers, turbans and other clothes, were bound and thrown into the blazing furnace. The king's command is so urgent and the furnace so hot that the flames kill the soldiers who take up Shadrach, Meshach and Abednego, and these three men, firmly tied, fell into the blazing furnace.[70]

Silence falls across the land as news gets out that these boys have been thrown into the furnace. These popular young men that everyone likes have been executed. No more hope for them. They lived a short, but good life. Women are weeping, men hang their heads in disbelief wondering what

---

[69] Daniel 3:16-18
[70] Daniel 3:19-23

might have been. Some are dealing with guilt. They know they should have taken the stand with these men, but they were too cowardly to do so. It was easier to bow.

We have not reached the end of the story yet, but let me take just a little space to tell you that Christians all around the world are faced with this same dilemma every day. Their stories don't necessarily end like that of the three Hebrew young men, but their miracles are no less. Even in death they have squeezed a camel through. Paul said that "to live is Christ and to die is gain" [71]

According to many sources, a Christian loses his/her life every five minutes because of their faith. We must be willing to live for Jesus. Are you prepared to die for him? I know that's heavy; probably the heaviest part of this entire book, but it must be said. It must be asked. We, in western culture, are soft. We don't understand what our brothers and sisters in other nations are going through.

Shadrach, Meshach and Abednego's story ends happily.

Then King Nebuchadnezzar leaped to his feet in amazement and asked his advisers,

"Weren't there three men that we tied up and threw into the fire?"

They replied, "Certainly, O king."

He said, "Look! I see four men walking around in the fire, unbound and unharmed, and the fourth looks like a son of God."

Nebuchadnezzar then approached the opening of the blazing furnace and shouted,

"Shadrach, Meshach and Abednego, servants of the Most High God, come out! Come here!"

---

[71] Philippians 1:21

So Shadrach, Meshach and Abednego came out of the fire, and the satraps, prefects, governors and royal advisers crowded around them. They saw that the fire had not harmed their bodies, nor was a hair of their heads singed; their robes were not scorched, and there was no smell of fire on them.

Then Nebuchadnezzar said, "Praise be to the God of Shadrach, Meshach and Abednego, who has sent his angel and rescued his servants! They trusted in him and defied the king's command and were willing to give up their lives rather than serve or worship any god except their own God. Therefore I decree that the people of any nation or language who say anything against the God of Shadrach, Meshach and Abednego be cut into pieces and their houses be turned into piles of rubble, for no other god can save in this way."

Then the king promoted Shadrach, Meshach and Abednego in the province of Babylon.[72]

Shadrach, Meshach and Abednego got their camel through the eye of the needle because they had courage. They had the courage to stand when everyone else was bowing. They had the courage to refuse a second chance to bow. They had the courage to die for what they believed in.

The first miracle was complete when they were tossed into the furnace. Live or die, they were a miracle of faith.

The second miracle came in the furnace.

The Third miracle came when Nebuchadnezzar made a proclamation that no one was to ever say anything against the God of these boys.

---

[72] Daniel 3:24-30

Trust God with your difficult decisions. Believe that He is able to bring you through your circumstances. Believe that what looks impossible to you *is not* impossible with God.

Chapter Fourteen

Failure

Peter has a special place in Jesus' heart. They are friends. Peter is not only one of Jesus' twelve disciples, he has made it into the inner circle of three. What is it about Peter that Jesus loves so much? Is it the fact that he is rough around the edges and real? Peter is a commercial fisherman. Even at his young age, his skin is dark, weathered, leathery and wrinkled. His hair is slightly lighter because he has spent so much of his life in the sun. The many hours he has spent with his hands around heavy nets pulling them back into a boat loaded down with fish has left his hands calloused and rough. He is an outdoorsman. He is a 'man's man' and there is something unique about him that causes him to find favor with Jesus.

Peter has been a part of the team from the beginning of Jesus' ministry. He witnessed the very first miracle when Jesus turned water into wine at a wedding feast. Surely he was amazed and shocked beyond belief;

but *that* miracle was nothing compared to things that he would see in the next three years.

During his tenure as part of the Messiah's team, Peter witnessed the miraculous feeding of thousands with just a few fish and a little bread. He was a firsthand witness when Jesus resurrected the dead. One of those times, a man named Lazarus had been dead so long that he smelled dead. He witnessed the lepers being cleansed, the blind receiving their sight, and demon-possessed people being set free. He was in a boat with Jesus when a storm came; a storm so violent that the disciples thought they were about to die. Jesus lifted his hands above the water and told it to be still and immediately the storm stopped. He and the others were amazed. They asked each other "what kind of man this is, that the winds and the sea obey His voice."[73]

Peter was present for every teaching that Jesus did. He was a member of the congregation when Jesus preached the Sermon on the Mount. Peter is famous because he is an important part of Jesus' team.

In spite of his resume and life experiences, Peter is about to experience what could be considered, life-shattering failure. In a moment when Jesus will need his friends to stand up for Him, to identify with Him, to declare their solidarity with Him, Peter will fail. Jesus prepared Peter for this failure in advance, but Peter refused to believe that he, Peter, could fail so miserably. He replied,

"Even if all fall away on account of you, I never will."

"I tell you the truth," Jesus answered, "This very night, before the rooster crows, you will disown me three times."

But Peter declared, "Even if I have to die with you, I will never disown you." And all the other disciples said the same.[74]

---

[73] Matthew 4:37-41

The thought that he would deny Jesus is inconceivable to Peter. Jesus is his teacher, leader and best friend. "Even if I have to die with you, I will never disown you," he said. What he didn't know was that he would see things differently when the pressure was on.

Isn't that the way it is in our lives? When things are going smoothly, it's easy to make big promises. Things tend to change when we find ourselves under the intense heat of temptation or fear.

Decision day has come. Jesus is wrongfully arrested and put on trial. Three times Peter is questioned by those who recognize him. "Aren't you one of His followers?" Three times Peter denies that he knows Jesus. What must be going through his mind with each denial? What is the mental torment like? This is his best friend. He loves Jesus, but he's afraid. He's afraid that by identifying with Jesus, he might face the same arrest, the same torment, and the same public ridicule. By the time the third person questions Peter, his nerves are raw with agitation, disappointment, and guilt. He is aggravated and wants to be left alone. He curses and denies Jesus for the third time. The rooster crows, Jesus turns, looks at Peter and their eyes meet. Peter quickly looks away. He's ashamed! He moans loudly in disbelief. He can't believe it. He can't believe that he has actually denied Jesus. Peter gets up from his fireside seat. He feels as though he will explode with painful emotions.

He doesn't want anyone to see him. He runs, looking for a private alley. When he finds a spot, he falls to the ground and weeps bitterly.
He's a man. He's tough. He's never wept so deeply, so bitterly.[75]

It's the first real test that he's had as a follower of Jesus. He remembers with sorrow how Jesus told him that he would do this, and with

---

[74] Matthew 26:33
[75] Luke 22:60-22

even more sorrow he remembers his proclamation that he was willing to die with Jesus. *He is a failure.*

Where is the camel and the eye of the needle in all this? I'll get to that, but first, let me ask you a simple question. Have you failed at something? Have you declared that you were going to accomplish something just to have it all come crashing down around you in a heap of miserable failure?

Is your walk with the Lord one of misery because of guilt? You want so badly to serve God and give Him your best, but for whatever reason, you keep blowing it. Have you been like Peter, weeping because you were ashamed of your actions or lack of actions? There is forgiveness for you. Grace is available. I'll talk more about grace later.

Have you decided to never fall in love again because of a failed relationship and the pain that came with that? Have you decided that you will never step out in faith again because when you did, you think you were left looking foolish?

I have good news! First, you can get up from failure and try again. There is an old adage that says "winners never quit and quitters never win". I could spend a whole chapter dealing with people throughout history who failed miserably before accomplishing something great. I guess I'll mention a few. Even though most of these are examples of natural failure, there is a great spiritual lesson to be learned, so keep an open mind.

"Henry Ford: While Ford is known today for his innovative assembly line and American made cars, he wasn't an instant success. In fact, his early businesses failed and left him broke five times before he founded the successful Ford Motor Company".[76]

---

[76] Onlinecollege.org

"Bill Gates: Gates didn't seem like a shoe-in for success after dropping out of Harvard and starting a failed first business with Microsoft co-founder Paul Allen called Traf-O-Data. While this early idea didn't work, Gates' later work did, creating the global empire that is Microsoft."[77]

"Harland David Sanders: Perhaps better known as Colonel Sanders of Kentucky Fried Chicken fame, Sanders had a hard time selling his chicken at first. In fact, his famous secret chicken recipe was rejected 1,009 times before a restaurant accepted it."[78]

"Winston Churchill: This Nobel Prize-winning, twice-elected Prime Minister of the United Kingdom wasn't always as well regarded as he is today. Churchill struggled in school and failed the sixth grade. After school he faced many years of political failures, as he was defeated in every election for public office until he finally became the Prime Minister at the ripe old age of 62."[79]

Abraham Lincoln is one of my favorite people when it comes to the subject of overcoming multiple failures in life; so I'm going to take a little more space with him.

"Probably the greatest example of persistence is Abraham Lincoln. If you want to learn about somebody who didn't quit, look no further.

Born into poverty, Lincoln was faced with defeat throughout his life. He lost eight elections, twice failed in business and suffered a nervous breakdown.

He could have quit many times- but he didn't and because he didn't quit, he became one of the greatest presidents in the history of our country.

Lincoln was a champion and he never gave up. Here is a sketch of Lincoln's road to the White House:

---

[77] Ibid.
[78] Ibid.
[79] Ibid.

- 1816: His family was forced out of their home. He had to work to support them.
- 1818: His mother died.
- 1831: Failed in business.
- 1832: Ran for state legislature –LOST.
- 1832: Also lost his job – wanted to go to law school but couldn't get in.
- 1833: Borrowed some money from a friend to begin a business and by the end of the year he was bankrupt. He spent the next 17 years of his life paying off this debt.
- 1834: Ran for state legislature again –WON.
- 1835: Was engaged to be married, sweetheart died and his heart was broken.
- 1836: Had a total nervous breakdown and was in bed for six months.
- 1838: Sought to become speaker of the state legislature – LOST.
- 1843: Ran for Congress – LOST.
- 1846: Ran for Congress again – this time he WON – went to Washington and did a good job.
- 1848: Ran for re-election to Congress – LOST.
- 1849: Sought the job of land officer in his home state – REJECTED.
- 1854: Ran for Senate of the United States – LOST.
- 1856: Sought the Vice-Presidential nomination at his party's national convention – got less than 100 votes.
- 1858: Ran for U.S. Senate again – again he lost.
- 1860: Elected president of the United States.[80]

---

[80] Snopes.com

My final example of someone who overcame devastating failure is a man named Peter. Do you remember him? There's no failure worse than failing God. There is no failure more painful than when you let down the One that you love more than any other. Peter has traveled with Jesus for three years and declared an allegiance that he would be true to Jesus even in death. In one night, everything fell apart. It was bad enough that Jesus had been arrested and was being tried for a crime. I'm sure Peter was wondering what would come of his teacher and friend. Now, within a matter of a very short time, Peter is given three opportunities to identify himself with his friend; three opportunities to take a stand; three opportunities to do what he said he would do: die with his friend. All three times, he failed. When he hears the rooster crowing, the magnitude of what he has done hits home. The crow of the rooster doesn't seem normal. It's louder, more intense than any crow he has ever heard. It's like a bell ringing in his head. With the crow of the rooster, he sees and feels the eyes of Jesus, his friend. With the crow of the rooster, he feels like every eye in the world is looking at him and everyone knows exactly what he has done. There's nothing left to do but run.

Not long before this dreadful night, Peter and the other disciples had debated about who would sit next to Jesus when He came into His kingdom. Surely, before this horrible night, Peter believed that he had at least a one in three shot. Now he has failed the test. Now there's no hope for him. His sorrow, his misery, his agony must be about the same as what Judas felt after betraying Jesus.

There seemed to be no hope. To rise back into favor with Jesus, be a part of His team and play a role in His kingdom was now IMPOSSIBLE. A comeback would be like putting a camel through the eye of a needle.

There was an important subject that Peter was yet to know anything about. It would be the very foundation of Jesus' kingdom. That subject is grace, and Peter was about to experience exactly what grace is.

I don't know when it happened, but after Jesus' death, Peter just seems to fall into "grace" with Him. Suddenly, he's part of the picture again. Maybe he and Jesus had a conversation after the resurrection and Jesus told Peter he was forgiven; I'm not sure.

After Jesus ascended back to heaven, Peter was among those who, at the instruction of Jesus, gathered into an upper room to *"wait for the promise."* Here is this rough outdoorsman who has cursed and denied that he knew Jesus, and now he's waiting for the promise of the Holy Spirit. Amazing, isn't it? It's amazing grace! On the day of Pentecost, the promise came. It was the outpouring of the Holy Spirit, the birth of the New Testament church; and this failure of a man was there; he was part of it. Not only was he part of it but he, the failure, the man who just a short time earlier had cursed while denying that he even knew Jesus, now preaches the first sermon of the New Testament church.

Here is an account of the end of that sermon and the response of the people.

"Therefore let all Israel be assured of this: God has made this Jesus, whom you crucified, both Lord and Christ." When the people heard this, they were cut to the heart and said to Peter and the other apostles, "Brothers, what shall we do?" Peter replied, "Repent and be baptized, every one of you, in the name of Jesus Christ for the forgiveness of your sins. And you will receive the gift of the Holy Spirit. The promise is for you and your children and for all who are far off — for all whom the Lord our God will call." With many other words he warned them; and he pleaded with them, "Save yourselves from this corrupt generation." Those who accepted his message were baptized, and about three thousand were added to their number that day. [81]

I've been preaching and teaching the Word for twenty-eight years and I've never had a response anywhere near three thousand. I think it's safe to say that from the night Peter cursed in denying Jesus until the Day of Pentecost, a camel was squeezed through the eye of a needle in Peter's life.

Failure does not have to be the end. As a matter of fact, it can be the beginning of something new and prosperous. Remember the adage I shared with you earlier: "Winners never quit and quitters never win." Receive the grace of God in your life. Walk in His grace. Get up and try again. Like a toddler learning to walk, take baby steps. When you stumble, get up and try again.

Moral and spiritual failure may leave you feeling like God could never use you again. I want you to know that the same grace Peter experienced is available for you today. When we fail, God forgives us and he chooses to erase our failure from his memory bank. Get up from the depths of a spiritual pity party and quit making excuses. *Failure is not permission to quit; it's a mandate to try again.*

---

[81] Acts 2:36-41

Chapter Fifteen

Faith

Now faith is being sure of what we hope for and certain of what we do not see.[82]

Jesus spoke of faith the size of a mustard seed. So what is faith and how do we get it? If I can move mountains with it, I want it. The word "faith" that Jesus referred to and the word "faith" in Hebrews 11:1 come from the same Greek word, "pistis (pis'-tis)" and it means "to be persuaded; have a moral conviction or a reliance upon Christ" [83]

So if I have persuasion or reliance upon Christ just the size of a mustard seed, I can move mountains. I think I said this earlier but it bears repeating. It's one thing to say that you believe, it's quite another to actually believe.

---

[82] Hebrews 11:1
[83] PC Study Bible

How do you get this faith?

Consequently, faith comes from hearing the message, and the message is heard through the word of Christ. [84]

I love how the KJV translates this verse:

Rom 10:17 So then faith cometh by hearing, and hearing by the word of God.[85]

Jeff Scurlock Paraphrase: Faith comes by hearing the word of God.

The scripture makes it sound way too simple. Surely there is something else I have to do to have this faith. Well, not really. Let me break it down for you in a way I would break an outline down for one of my messages.

I. Become born again.

    A. Admit you're separated from God because of sin.

    B. Accept the work of Jesus at Calvary.

    Rom 3:23

    for all have sinned and fall short of the glory of God,

    C. Repent or turn away from your sin: To repent means to turn around and walk in a different direction.

    Acts 3:19

    Repent, then, and turn to God, so that your sins may be wiped out...

II. Confess Jesus as Lord.

    Rom 10:9-11

    9 That if you confess with your mouth, "Jesus is Lord," and believe in your heart that God raised him from the dead, you

---

[84] Romans 10:17-18
[85] Romans 10:17 KJV

will be saved. 10 For it is with your heart that you believe and are justified, and it is with your mouth that you confess and are saved.

III. Become part of a local church.
IV. The church is the body of Christ and as a believer, you should be a part of it.
V. Help your church.
      i. With your attendance.
      ii. With your finances.
      iii. With your skills.
      iv. With your encouragement.
      v. With your fasting and prayer
      vi. Not necessarily in that order.
VI. Hear the Word of God
      i. Why? Because that's how you build your faith.
      ii. How?
          Read your Bible every day.
          Study your Bible.
          Memorize Scripture.
VII. Go to a small group such as a Sunday School class at your church.
      i. Go to church and listen to the teachings from your pastor.
      ii. Read Christian books by good, solid authors.
      iii. Listen to podcasts of good teaching.
      iv. Listen to the Bible on podcast.
      v. Do everything you can to get as much of the Word in you as possible.

VIII.   Declare what you believe, based on what you have heard.
IX.   Say what the Word says.
X.   Say what you believe.

Sounds pretty simple doesn't it? Then why is it so hard for some? I propose to you that it's hard because of a lack of faithfulness to the steps above. As I stated earlier in this book, many are religious, but have never begun a personal relationship with Jesus. How on earth does that person expect to use faith to move mountains, or squeeze a camel through the eye of a needle when they will not use faith to trust in Jesus as their savior? Go to God in prayer now. Ask him to forgive you of all your sins, come into your life and be your Lord. Make up your mind today that from this day forward you will not be just religious, but that you will be a follower of Jesus! Amen and Amen!!

Instead of going to church, some stay home and watch television or do some other activity that is more important to them than being at church. Church is something that some people do when they have nothing better to do. Frankly, there should never be anything more important to you on a Sunday morning or Bible Study night than being at your Bible-teaching church where you will be taught and equipped to have faith. And, don't just go to church. Be a viable part of your church. Be an encourager. Be a worker and a giver. *You can make a difference in your church and God will use your church to make a difference in you!*

It's hard because the Word of God does not have the place of importance in lives that it should have. The Bible is viewed by many, even some Christians, as "the good book." It's something that we need in our lives to help us stay good and please "the man upstairs." WRONG!

WRONG! WRONG! The Bible is the inerrant, infallible, Holy Spirit inspired, living and life-giving Word of God.

If your view of the Bible is that it's old, dusty, and boring, you will never have the faith it takes to accomplish great things for God, trying to squeeze a camel through the eye of a needle; not until you change your view of scripture.

If your view of the Bible is that it's out of date and irrelevant, then you are WRONG! If you think the Bible is something that's only important when you're in trouble, then you will stay in trouble.

Neglecting your relationship with God and his Word will get your butt kicked; and you will wonder what happened.

Some Jews who went around driving out evil spirits tried to invoke the name of the Lord Jesus over those who were demon-possessed. They would say, "In the name of Jesus, whom Paul preaches, I command you to come out." Seven sons of Sceva, a Jewish chief priest, were doing this. [One day] the evil spirit answered them, "Jesus I know, and I know about Paul, but who are you?" Then the man who had the evil spirit jumped on them and overpowered them all. He gave them such a beating that they ran out of the house naked and bleeding.[86]

There is authority in being a child of God, but there will be embarrassment if you try to fake it.

Let the Word of God come alive for you and in you. If you can't understand the King James Version of the Bible, that's alright, get a modern translation. Please understand me. I love the King James Bible. I grew up on it and most of the time when I'm quoting scripture it's scripture that I memorized in King James. However, you will notice that in this book, I have used mostly translations that are more modern than the KJV. Why?

---

[86] Acts 19:13-16

Because I want everyone to understand the message. Because I want you to know that you don't have to speak the King's English from 1611 to have a relationship with God. So I'll say it again with much conviction: if you can't understand the Bible you have, find you a modern translation (not a paraphrase), read it and let it come alive in your life.

Learn to quote Bible verses to your situation. After Jesus had fasted for forty days, Satan came to tempt him. With every temptation of the devil, Jesus declared the Word of God. He would say "It is written," and then quote a scripture. The Word of God is powerful. We need to hear ourselves quote it because it reinforces our faith. Our enemy needs to hear us quote it because it's our sword.

Finally, be strong in the Lord and in his mighty power. Put on the full armor of God so that you can take your stand against the devil's schemes. For our struggle is not against flesh and blood, but against the rulers, against the authorities, against the powers of this dark world and against the spiritual forces of evil in the heavenly realms. Therefore put on the full armor of God, so that when the day of evil comes, you may be able to stand your ground, and after you have done everything, to stand. Stand firm then, with the belt of truth buckled around your waist, with the breastplate of righteousness in place, and with your feet fitted with the readiness that comes from the gospel of peace. In addition to all this, take up the shield of faith, with which you can extinguish all the flaming arrows of the evil one. Take the helmet of salvation and the sword of the Spirit, which is the word of God.[87]

I debated with myself as to whether or not I needed to share all of the above scripture. I decided that it was vital for me to make my point about "speaking" the Word of God. This segment of Ephesians 6 is about spiritual

---

[87] Ephesians 6:10-18

warfare. We are encouraged to "be strong in the Lord" and then put on the armor of God. Every piece of armor is defensive. It's there to protect. What I want you to see is in verse seventeen where Paul says "Take the helmet of salvation and the *sword of the Spirit, which is the word of God."* A sword can be used defensively, but it's also the only offensive weapon in Ephesians 6. When the enemy comes at you with doubt and unbelief, use the Word to defend your faith, and use the Word to go on the attack. Declare what the Bible says. Use it to declare what your life will be.

Learn to speak your dreams. Say what you're dreaming or believing God for and don't listen to the detractors or distracters. Find scriptures that encourage your faith or speak directly into your situation. Print those scriptures out in bold lettering and then put them all over your house in prominent places. Learn them, memorize them, say them over and over. Speak to your mountains. Declare what Jesus said, "With men this is impossible, but with God all things are possible."[88]

When God puts a call in your heart, tell people who will encourage you and stay away from those who are negative and will discourage you. It makes you more determined to see it through when you broadcast it to the world. It also builds your faith to hear yourself saying, "God has called me to believe and I have answered that call."

---

[88] Matthew 19:26

Chapter Sixteen
Challenges

A person who is determined to 'stay safe' won't be used by God to their fullest potential. The challenge before us is to answer the call of God even if it's scary. The call of God will not necessarily come in a voice or even a sign. Many times it comes in the form of a need that someone must step up and meet or a challenge that presents itself. Sometimes it is the voice of the Holy Spirit calling your name and asking, "Will you go?"

A champion named Goliath, who is from Gath, came out of the Philistine camp. He is over nine feet tall. He has a bronze helmet on his head and is wearing a coat of scale armor of bronze weighing five thousand shekels; on his legs he is wearing bronze greaves, and a bronze javelin is slung on his back. His spear shaft is like a weaver's rod, and its iron point weighs six hundred shekels. His shield bearer goes ahead of him. Goliath stands and shouts to the ranks of Israel,

"Why do you come out and line up for battle? Am I not a Philistine, and are you not the servants of Saul? Choose a man and have him come down to me. If he is able to fight and kill me, we will become your subjects; but if I overcome him and kill him, you will become our subjects and serve us."

Then the Philistine said,

"This day I defy the ranks of Israel! Give me a man and let us fight each other." On hearing the Philistine's words, Saul and all the Israelites were dismayed and terrified.[89]

Young David sees the challenge. It was a giant. It is the Philistine champion Goliath, who stands before the army of Israel and makes fun of them because no one has the courage or enough faith in God to face him in a one-on-one battle. Seasoned soldiers cower and walk away from this giant of a challenge.

David, who is the youngest of his father's sons, is not a soldier in the army. He is a shepherd boy. The only reason he's even near the battle field is because his father sent him to check on the welfare of his brothers. He is not there to join the army, not there to fight any battles. But, a challenge has presented itself.

David asks the men standing near him, "What will be done for the man who kills this Philistine and removes this disgrace from Israel? Who is this uncircumcised Philistine that he should defy the armies of the living God?" [90]

Apparently David already has his mind made up. He hasn't said it yet, but he is asking the right question, "What will be done for the man who kills this Philistine?" He wants to know what was going to be in it for him.

---

[89] 1 Samuel 17:4-11
[90] 1 Samuel 17:26

Maybe he is a little arrogant, but he sees a challenge and he is going to do something about it.

This is a lesson that we, the people of God, need to learn to ask. We need to see the challenges that face the church of Jesus Christ and be willing to step up to the plate to take on these challenges. I learned years ago that when someone came to me with a concern or the vision for a ministry, to say, "That sounds great, do it!" or, "You take care of it." They usually look like they have been shot between the eyes. People see the challenges, the needs and even have visions for ministries, but they want someone else to do it and usually they have their pastor in mind. After all, he's in this ministry business full-time.

Dr. Mel Ming is a brilliant church leader, college professor, church consultant and former pastor. I heard him say in a meeting just a few days ago, talking to pastors, "God has a plan for your life, so does everyone else." Your pastor does not need you to bring him another challenge unless you plan to help find the solution and you plan to play a great role in that solution.

People of God, step up to the challenge. The challenge presented is a call for you! God is calling you to work, believe and achieve big, seemingly impossible things for Him. He's calling you to use that tiny, mustard seed size faith for Him.

David made the right declaration with another question, "Who is this uncircumcised Philistine that he should defy the armies of the living God?" What he was saying was, "Who does the devil think he is? Does Goliath have the spiritual authority to defy God's army? No!"

Have we given Satan the authority to defy what the Bible says and thereby keep us from living the life that the Word says is ours? If so, it's time to take our stand and declare what God's Word says. Is Satan standing before you and defying God's Word? I promise you, if he's not, he will. There is a challenge before you. It's called spiritual warfare.

God has put calls, visions and dreams in your life and there are reasons why they have not come to pass. It could be laziness, but most of the time, at least in my experiences, it's because of the spiritual war. It could also be because of the rants of the Goliaths of our lives and the lack of a willingness to fight a battle.

It's easier to stay back in the camp. It's easier to stay in Egypt than to possess the promise of God. It's easier to live without faith.

Earlier, I quoted Oswald Chambers from his book, *My Utmost for His Highest*. I think I should repeat it. "It's easier to serve God without a vision, easier to work for God without a call, because then you are not bothered by what God requires; common sense is your guide, veneered over with Christian sentiment. You will be more successful, more leisure-hearted, if you never realize the call of God. But if once you receive a commission in Jesus Christ, the memory of what God wants will always come like a goad; you will no longer be able to work for Him on the common sense basis."[91]

If you live by the code of easy, you will be visionless; you will never really experience the joy of working for God with a call. It will be easier, according to Chambers, because you won't be bothered by God.

"Noah, I have instructions for you," God said. What if Noah's response was, "I'd rather not be bothered, even by God?"

People attend church, pray and make sure God has their laundry list of needs without ever one time asking God what they can do for Him. I wonder what it will be like for them when they stand before Christ and have to admit that they wasted the life that was given to them.

---

[91] Oswald Chambers, *My Utmost for His Highest*. (Westwood, NJ: Barbour and Co., 1963).

Then there are those who have answered the call; they have received a commission. "The memory of what God wants will always come like a goad," according to Chambers. I have to admit that I didn't know what a goad is, so I visited dictionary.com and learned that a goad is a stick with something sharp on the end of it or even an electrical charge that is used to keep livestock moving. Now I understand a goad.

When I was in high school, I was a member of the FFA, the Future Farmers of America. I had no plan to be a farmer, but it was required that we join FFA if we wanted to be in shop class. I wanted to be in shop class because it was an easy 'A' and more of a place to hang out for an hour than other classes where you had to actually study and learn.

During my tenure in the FFA, I became interested in the competition of 'showing livestock.' My livestock of choice was a calf. It was a competition where you took a calf you raised to show at a 'show' and were judged. The calf was to be clean, groomed and trained to walk beside the person showing it.

My lifelong friend, David, and I were partners in this venture, with the help of his dad. David's dad had the items we needed: the farm, the money, the cattle, and the calves. It was his investment, not ours. All we had to do was prepare these animals for the show which were ultimately to be sold in auction. The most important part of the show was having that calf walk with you like a trained pup.

Our first day of training these animals, David prepared me for what was about to happen. At least he thought he did. The calf was put into a chute where its head was locked down and a harness and rope attached. David prepared me by having me hold the rope with it wrapped around my hand, ready for a battle with this calf. I was told that this eight hundred pound animal would drag me all over the barnyard but that I couldn't give in. It would be a battle of the wills. He told me to use objects such as trees and poles to wrap the rope around and stare this beast down to let it know who was boss. I wasn't concerned in the least. I was a champion power-lifter, remember?

The moment came. With the rope firmly in hand, my boots dug into the ground and my posture in a pulling stance, I gave the word for this beast to be released. The gate opened.........nothing. Nothing happened. The calf didn't' come rushing out ready to defeat me in the battle of man vs. beast. It just stood there, looked at me and said, "Moo." Moo? I was so upset, disappointed and even angry. I was ready for a battle but instead received a gentle moo. David said that this was highly unusual, but reassured me that once we got the calf to leave the chute, the battle would be on. After what seemed like hours of pulling and pushing, the calf finally left the safety of the chute and stepped into the barnyard with me. Still there was no battle. Nothing! Over the next several days, we did everything we could think of to get that stubborn calf to walk with me. Nothing worked.

One day, David's dad tied the rope attached to the calf to the bumper of his truck. Before I tell you the rest of this story, you have to promise not to tell the crazies at PETA! It was 1977! We would never do this now (wink). He tied the rope to the bumper of the truck and then started driving very slowly. You would have been amazed at the determination of this animal. It dug its hooves into the ground and tried to keep that truck from moving. When it realized that it couldn't stop the movement, it laid on its side and allowed the truck to drag it. Still, this stubborn animal refused to walk.

I realize that I'm taking way too much time and space to tell this story but there is a point, *literally*.

David's dad got an idea. "Oh my," he said. "Why didn't I think of this sooner?" Mine and David's interest was piqued. He had our attention. "What?" we asked. "Boys, I'll be right back." The suspense was killing me as he disappeared into the barn. I could hear sounds like he was digging around, looking for something. I finally heard him say, "There it is!" When he reappeared from the barn, he had a gadget in his hand. It was about the length of a golf club. It had a red handle, a white shaft and a red tip. "Jeffrey," he said. "Grab that rope and hang on." He walked up behind that calf, stuck that gadget to its rear and pushed a button on the handle. I heard the sound of an electrical buzz. *Now this animal was moving*! The battle that I had so longed for was on, for about thirty seconds. He's just standing there again; he turns his head toward me and gives me that, *"why,"* look. David's dad touched him again, same sound, same results for about the same amount of time. We did this day after day, hoping this calf would get the point on its own.

The gadget that David's dad was using was a Hot Shot. It was a modern day goad!

The day of the show finally came and by that point I had it all figured out. We couldn't have anyone follow us with the Hot Shot, but it wasn't necessary. By this time, I had the calf where it would walk with me but if it even hesitated, all I had to do was to make the buzzing sound with my mouth that the Hot Shot made and the calf would kick back into gear and walk.

Now I understand what Oswald Chambers meant when he said, "if once you receive a commission in Jesus Christ, the memory of What God wants will always come like a goad." It means that once you see the challenge and accept it as the call of God, you will be shocked back into reality by the call when you forget, look away or stop walking.

Is there a challenge before you that is goading you? Do you have a call from God that you would rather just forget, but it pushes you like a goad?

David knew that the giant who was cursing God's army was his challenge, his calling. It was a calling that he met head on. He used the talent he had and took the giant down.

What is the challenge that you see? What is the calling that is before you? Has God called you to leave the comfort of 'normal' and step into the realm of the seemingly impossible challenge? Do you see life's mountains as challenges that are to be overcome? They are! Don't take the easy route. Don't be lazy and afraid to step up and meet your challenge head on. Remember the words of Jesus:

"I tell you the truth, if you have faith as small as a mustard seed, you can say to this mountain, 'Move from here to there' and it will move. Nothing will be impossible for you." [92]

Jesus looked at the disciples and said, "With man this is impossible, but with God all things are possible." [93]

---

[92] Matthew 17:20
[93] Matthew 19:26

Chapter Seventeen
Help Is On the Way

I'm sure that if you watch any television at all, you've seen the "Lifeline" commercial. A lady is lying on the floor, injured. Around her neck is a chain with an electronic pendant. She mashes the button on the pendant which connects her with help. Once she knows for a fact that she is connected with that help she says, "Help! I've fallen and I can't get up!" to which the voice on the other end says, "Help is on the way."

I've shared several stories with you that are a testimonies of triumph over tragedy and faith over hopelessness; stories that encourage us to believe in God, believe in ourselves and to work hard.

If you have taken these stories to be some type of self-help, mind over matter, power of positive thinking remedies for life's problems, you have missed the point all together. So, I want to make sure before this book is laid to rest in a bookshelf somewhere, that you understand its purpose.

There is no victory in the life of a believer apart from a relationship with God and a dependency on His authority and power. In the first scripture we used, Jesus said in rebuke of his disciples, "If you had the faith the size of a mustard seed, nothing would be impossible for you."

Well, the question has to be posed, faith in what? If you don't know the answer to that question, you will put your faith in the wrong things, and that's dangerous. Some might think that it's faith in yourself. NO! Some might think that it's faith in the power of the mind. NO! Some might think that it has something to do with a perfect balance of the "yin and yang." NO!

When Jesus declared a need for faith to his disciples, He meant faith in God. Faith in God is an absolute necessity in our relationship with Him. Faith in God is an absolute necessity when facing challenges or overcoming obstacles.

I talked about David and the challenge of Goliath. I need to make sure that I make this point. David's confidence, in facing Goliath, had nothing to do with the skill he had with a sling. He knew he was good with the sling. He also knew that without God, he was in trouble.

And Saul said to David,

"You are not able to go against this Philistine to fight with him; for you are a youth, and he a man of war from his youth."

But David said to Saul,

"Your servant used to keep his father's sheep, and when a lion or a bear came and took a lamb out of the flock, I went out after it and struck it, and delivered the lamb from its mouth; and when it arose against me, I caught it by its beard, and struck and killed it. Your servant has killed both lion and bear; and this uncircumcised Philistine will be like one of them, seeing he has defied the armies of the living God." Moreover, David said,

"The Lord, who delivered me from the paw of the lion and from the paw of the bear, He will deliver me from the hand of this Philistine."[94]

David knew where his help was coming from. It amazes me how people tend to get real cocky or self-absorbed and throw their chest out when they have some success. Don't forget where your help comes from, and be sure to give God the credit.

When Jesus was discussing how difficult it was for a rich man to go to heaven, He related it to getting a camel through the eye of a needle and indicated that it was an impossible thing to do, except by God.

All of these individuals that we have talked about would declare to you that they would not have succeeded without the help of God. God's help in this life is absolutely necessary. You will not have the comfort of His help without absolute faith in Him.

Have you ever cried out to God in desperation, "Help! I've fallen and I can't get up?" Have you felt as though you would not make it through the day if God didn't come to your side and help you? Good. We need to know that we need the help of God.

With God in the equation, we get much more done and He gets way more credit.

If something great has happened in your life, you had some help. If you take all the credit, you're not as smart as you think you are.

Alex Haley, the author of the novel *Roots: The Saga of an American Family*, which was later turned into one of the most successful television mini-series of all time, had a picture of a turtle on top of a fence post in his office and he would say, "If a turtle is on top of a post, he had some help."[95]

---

[94] 1 Samuel 17:33-37
[95] www.bible.org/illustration/alex-haley

If you have rallied your faith and have seen the realization of something thought to be impossible in your life, you had some help. If you are in a place right now where you feel like you're about to go under, you need to stir up your faith; you need some help. Cry out to God. He will answer.

God is our refuge and strength, an ever-present help in trouble.[96]

Truer words have never been spoken or penned. I could write in this book a word study on that scripture, but it's not necessary. It's perfectly clear. 'Refuge' means shelter and 'help' means to come to your aid. No matter what the dilemma is, there is help to be found in a relationship with God. "If you have faith (in God), nothing shall be impossible to you." If you can't get the camel through the eye of the needle, call on God because "with Him, *nothing is impossible*" or, "with Him, *anything is possible*."

In my distress I called to the Lord; I cried to my God for help. From his temple he heard my voice; my cry came before him, into his ears.[97]

In my alarm I said, "I am cut off from your sight!" Yet you heard my cry for mercy when I called to you for help. Love the Lord, all his saints! The Lord preserves the faithful, but the proud he pays back in full. Be strong and take heart, all you who hope in the Lord.[98]

Unless the Lord had given me help, I would soon have dwelt in the silence of death. When I said, "My foot is slipping," your love, O Lord, supported me. When anxiety was great within me, your consolation brought joy to my soul.[99]

Do you get my point, or maybe I should say, God's point? I could fill pages and pages of this book with nothing but scripture that tell of a God

---

[96] Psalms 46:1
[97] Psalms 18:6
[98] Psalms 31:22-24
[99] Psalms 94:17-19

who loves and helps those who trust in Him. How is it that a mom who has lost three children is still sane? Because in her distress, in her times of grief, when in the natural she should have been coming to pieces, her God whom she trusts came to her aid, and is continuing to be her help. He has become her refuge, her shelter, her hiding place.

Too many people are defeated because they trusted in Oprah or Doctor Phil. They have read the secular self-help books that have led them down a path of destruction and confusion. It's not that God doesn't love them. It's that they go in the wrong direction and put their confidence in wrong things.

The late Steve Jobs, co-founder of Apple, spent his whole life trying to find *enlightenment* through Eastern spirituality, Hinduism, and Zen Buddhism. "Throughout his life he would seek to follow the basic precepts of eastern religions, such as the emphasis on experiential prajna, wisdom or cognitive understanding that is intuitively experienced through concentration of the mind".[100] "Jobs's compulsive search for self-awareness also led him to undergo primal scream therapy."[101]

When Jobs discovered that he had cancer, he put much needed surgery off for nine months; a surgery that some believe would have saved his life. He put it off because he believed he could cure himself with Eastern spirituality and a Vegan diet."[102]

Steve Jobs lived a tormented life and died having never found his enlightenment or self-awareness.

What could Steve Jobs have accomplished as a believer? We'll never know.

Many times Christians put their confidence in the wrong things too.

---

[100] *Steve Jobs*, Copyright 2011 by Walter Isaacson: Simon & Schuster
[101] Ibid.,
[102] Ibid.,

Their priorities are way out of order. Instead of going to church and being taught how to live by faith, people stay in bed or go to the golf course. Instead of trusting God with their finances and bringing tithes and offerings into the storehouse, they buy lottery tickets, or try to find inner peace with shopping sprees. Anything other than trusting the God of the universe who created heaven and earth is a path of destruction.

Man is rejecting God and society feels the pain of destruction. There was a time when our country understood our need for God. Now, God is no longer welcome in public schools and in the town square. Holy conviction has given way to political correctness and the world suffers.

The decision that you have to make is between putting your trust in a secular society that rejects God or trusting God with everything.

Noah didn't have the support of his society. Except for the fact that he was putting money into the economy by hiring help for the construction job, he was thought to be a fool. He could have crumbled beneath the strain of being the town joke; instead, he decided to ignore the culture and obey God.

What will you do? How will you overcome your obstacles or the great challenges of life? Are you going to yell out to God for help?

I'll end this chapter with some helpful, but simple points to remember when facing a challenge.

- Recognize the challenge.
- Ask God for help. PRAY!
- Take a step of faith, and then another one.
- Walk by faith.
- When something good happens, give God all of the praise.
- Win in life.

Chapter Eighteen

How?

How can God do something as miraculous as putting a camel through the eye of a needle? Think about it. I've tried putting a tiny piece of thread through a needle and found that to be quite difficult for my delicate little hands. Jesus comes on the scene and says that the things in life that are impossible with man are possible with God.

All things are possible? What does "all" mean? It means all. It's possible for a camel to go through the eye of a needle because Jesus said it is. It's possible for cancers to dry up, for blind men to see, the deaf to hear and for a man who is lost in his transgressions to become clean through the grace of God and be born again.

In order to understand how God can do the miraculous in your life, you have to understand the enormity of who God is.

For by him all things were created: things in heaven and on earth, visible and invisible, whether thrones or powers or rulers or authorities; all things were created by him and for him.[103]

All things were created by Him. You, the camel and the needle. They were created by him and for him. He has complete control over all of his creation except man. Man was created as a free moral agent.

In his book, *Crazy Love,* Francis Chan said: "If my mind is the size of a soda can and God is the size of all the oceans, it would be stupid for me to say He is only the small amount of water I can scoop into my little can. God is so much bigger, so far beyond our time-encased, food and sleep dependant lives."[104]

In other words, even though there are scriptures that describe the bigness of God, we can't really comprehend how big He is. We try to figure God out by human reasoning in a brain the size of a soda can and God is so much bigger than the understanding that we can cram in there. This is why it's so important for us to believe and accept God on the basis of faith and know that His ways are different than ours.

"For my thoughts are not your thoughts, neither are your ways my ways," declares the Lord. "As the heavens are higher than the earth, so are my ways higher than your ways and my thoughts than your thoughts."[105]

God is saying that you can't figure Him out with only human reasoning. He's bigger, smarter, wiser, more powerful (all powerful) than anything, anyone or all the brain power of every person who has ever lived combined.

---

[103] Colossians 1:16
[104] *Crazy Love*, (Copyright 2008 by Francis Chan: David C. Cook)
[105] Isaiah 55:8-9

God is so powerful that it is impossible for him to lie. Whatever he speaks becomes the truth. I've often said that God could point to a white wall and say, "That wall is black," and it will be black. He's so powerful that he calls thing that are not as though they were and it becomes so.

Therefore, the promise comes by faith, so that it may be by grace and may be guaranteed to all Abraham's offspring — not only to those who are of the law but also to those who are of the faith of Abraham. He is the father of us all. As it is written: "I have made you a father of many nations." He is our father in the sight of God, in whom he believed — the God who gives life to the dead and calls things that are not as though they were. [106]

Look at the end of that scripture again. The God that I'm talking about "gives life to the dead and calls things that are not as though they were." How can God possibly get a camel through the eye of a needle? He declares it to be so and it is so.

Your dream is not too big for God. Go ahead and dream. I dare you to reach for something that is way beyond your capabilities. Ask God to help you bring your dream to pass. Don't be afraid to ask Him for big things. I heard someone say recently, "God is not offended by big requests, He's offended by anything less."

"It is absolutely imperative at the outset that you come to terms with this simple yet life-changing truth: God is for you. If you don't believe that, then you'll pray small timid prayers; if you do believe it, then you'll pray big audacious prayers. And one way or another, your small timid prayers or big audacious prayers will change the trajectory of your life and turn you into two totally different people. Prayers are prophecies. They are the best predictors of your spiritual future. Who you become is determined by how

---

[106] Romans 4:16-17

you pray. Ultimately, the transcript of your prayers becomes the script of your life."[107]

Your calling may look impossible to you, but nothing is too big or beyond the realm of possibilities with God. Quit trying to limit Him to what you can get into your brain (the soda can). Try to look beyond yourself and at least make an attempt to understand that God is so big and so powerful there is nothing, *absolutely nothing*, that He cannot do.

I grew up in a singing family. My parents and their six children are all singers and musicians. My childhood was full of southern gospel singings. Many of the songs that I heard growing up have stuck with me. My parents sang a song by Dottie Rambo and Jimmie Davis. The chorus says:

"There is nothing, no nothing; there is nothing that my God can't do. Miracles and wonders, there is nothing, no nothing that my God can't do."

Your life challenges are not too big for God: sickness, financial needs, or whatever you're faced with. Would you please stop trying to beat every challenge with your extremely limited abilities and would you please get up from your pity party and put your confidence in God, who has declared His love for you throughout His Word.

You and I will never, in this life be able to completely comprehend God. I'm getting a little fuzzy in the head typing these words. That's why we must believe that He exists and that He has more power than our minds can comprehend.

And without faith it is impossible to please God, because anyone who comes to him must believe that he exists and that he rewards those who

---

[107] Mark Batterson, *The Circle Maker*, (Copyright 2011 by Mark Batterson: Zondervan)

earnestly seek him. [108]

I believed in God as a child because I was told to believe. It's easy for a child. You can tell a three year old that the moon is made out of cheese and they will be amazed. Children believe what they can't see simply because someone told them so. Jesus said that we have to be like children.

I tell you the truth, anyone who will not receive the kingdom of God like a little child will never enter it."[109]

Have the faith of a child. Believe like a child. Believe that God is so big and so beyond your ability to comprehend, but He is a personal God, and cares about your life, your battles, your victories, and your needs.

I'm not talking about being immature or mindless. The good news is, you don't have to check your brain at the door to serve God. What I'm talking about is simple faith.

You should also get acquainted with God intellectually. Approach Him with child-like faith and learn about Him with the brain He has given you. Study His Word. *Mature knowledge coupled with child-like faith is powerful.*

How does He do it? He's God! I could write pages and pages concerning the attributes and the abilities of God. I will give you just a few. God is unchangeable. God is eternal: He always has been and He always will be. God is omniscient: He knows everything, including the future. He is omnipotent: He's all-powerful and there is nothing He cannot do except lie or change. God is omnipresent: He is the only being, natural or spiritual who can be in all places at one time. God is: Faithful, Good, Holy, Impartial, Incomprehensible, Infinite, Longsuffering, Loving, Merciful, Righteous, True and the list goes on and on and on. He is totally Self-existent and Self-

---

[108] Hebrews 11:6
[109] Luke 18:17

sufficient. Only He can claim that. Why? Because, He is the only, real and living God.

He's the only living God and He wants you to trust Him. You will never (in this life) completely understand how God does what he does. Your part is to trust Him.

Conclusion

In the history of the Bible and of mankind apart from those in the Bible, there are hundreds of stories. There are real historical accounts of those who have risen out of the ashes of defeat to accomplish something substantial. This book would contain thousands of pages had I even tried to include them all.

I'm confident that the stories and Biblical accounts that I have shared in this book are adequate for my purpose of encouraging you to increase your resolve and build your faith. I understand that what you just read includes some stories that don't mention God or faith. My purpose in doing so was to remind you that in creating you, God has given you special gifts and talents that are at your disposal.

For you created my inmost being; you knit me together in my mother's womb. I praise you because I am fearfully and wonderfully made;[110]

You are wonderfully made. You are unique. There is not another person in the world who is alive right now, has lived in the past, or will ever live that was, is or will be exactly like you. When you look into the mirror, what you're looking at is God's creation. Maybe you don't like what you see. You wish you were skinnier, had more hair, had less hair, had different color eyes or that you were taller. There is a real tendency to never be satisfied with ourselves, how we look, how we sound, our level of intelligence, etc, etc, etc.

In 1965, the English rock band, *The Rolling Stones,* recorded and released a song entitled, "Satisfaction" or "I Can't Get No Satisfaction." The words in the title are repeated in the song multiple times. It sounds to me like the anthem of humankind. No Satisfaction! It rings truer today than ever before. People are looking to everything other than God for satisfaction and they are not finding it.

Take what you have, the abilities and talents that God has given you, and accomplish something big.

The second thing I want to bring to your attention concerning your abilities is that if you will take what you have and couple it together with your faith in God, mountains will move, camels will squeeze through the eye of a needle and your life will be a testimony to the greatness of God.

The last thing I want to point out is that there are people in this world who have no good looks, no great abilities or any special talents. I believe that people like us are on the top of God's list when He is looking for someone to get His work done. He's looking for people who are absolutely dependent on Him; people who stand completely on faith and nothing else.

---

[110] Psalms 139:13-14

Let me remind you that Dave Roever lost sixty percent of his flesh when that white phosphorus hand grenade exploded in his hand. He was left crippled and scarred beyond comprehension, but he is taking the life that he has *with the scars* and the pain and he's accomplishing great things for God.

Don't forget David Ring, whose face and motor skills are crippled by incurable cerebral palsy. Can you imagine what he had to endure growing up? How many people laughed at him or told him he was stupid or called him retarded (a bad word by the way). How many times did he fight the reality in his own mind that his life would never amount to anything because he was crippled? In spite of it all, David Ring took what he had, coupled it together with faith and has become a world-renowned evangelist.

What is your excuse? Are you letting the days of your life pass by without taking steps of faith to let God use you? You might have a good job, a spouse and kids, a nice home and go to church on Sunday. Wow! Is that it? Is that all you're going to do with your life? Are you kidding?

What are you going to say to Jesus when he asks you to explain what you did with your life?

"Well, Lord, I got a really good job and uh, Lord, I uh, married a beautiful woman and uhhhh I bought a house. You know, Lord, we lived in a really good neighborhood. I did want my life to bring you glory so I uh bought the nicest home and uh Lord I drove a really nice car. I always had a boat because uh, Lord I knew you liked uh… fishermen. Oh! And uh,… Lord I went to church on Sunday and uh… paid my tithes, uh… most of the time… I'd say, Lord, all in all, I think I did pretty good with the life you gave me."

I can hear the Lord's response.

"Ok, let me see if I've got this straight. You worked a job, married, bought a house, drove a nice car, always had a boat and you went to church and paid your tithes. Is that all?"

Are you going to feel the embarrassment of knowing that when everything was said and done, your life might have meant so much more? Will you be embarrassed that you backed down from every challenge?

As an English-speaking Indian pastor said, and asked his congregation the Sunday morning that I spoke in his church, "You have but one life to live, what will you do with yours?"

I'm asking you the same question. What will *you* do with *your* life or what's left of it? What big challenges will you take on? How many camels can you squeeze through the eye of a needle in the days, weeks and years to come? You have only one life. Use it for God's glory!

IN THE RIGHT HANDS, THIS BOOK WILL CHANGE LIVES

Most of the people who need this message will not be looking for this book. To change their lives, we ask that you put a copy of this book in their hands.

The mission of Jeff Scurlock is to find the good ground, the people who need this message, to change their lives. Will you help us reach these people?

You can order additional copies of this book at:
www.jeffscurlock.com
www.amazon.com

"This book will be a 'goad' in the spirit of many people to prod them toward the 'doing' of what God has already put in their hearts."

Renee Shipp, Editor

www.ingramcontent.com/pod-product-compliance
Lightning Source LLC
Chambersburg PA
CBHW061323040426
42444CB00011B/2751